Trespass – Summary Procedu
Possession of Land

Trespass – Summary Procedure for Possession of Land

Peter W. Birts, MA (Cantab)
Barrister of Gray's Inn

Alan Willis,
Solicitor

London
Butterworths
1987

United Kingdom	Butterworth & Co (Publishers) Ltd, 88 Kingsway, LONDON WC2B 6AB and 61A North Castle Street, EDINBURGH EH2 3LJ
Australia	Butterworths Pty Ltd, SYDNEY, MELBOURNE, BRISBANE, ADELAIDE, PERTH, CANBERRA and HOBART
Canada	Butterworths, A division of Reed Inc., TORONTO and VANCOUVER
New Zealand	Butterworths of New Zealand Ltd, WELLINGTON and AUCKLAND
Singapore	Butterworth & Co (Asia) Pte Ltd, SINGAPORE
South Africa	Butterworth Publishers (Pty) Ltd, DURBAN and PRETORIA
USA	Butterworths Legal Publishers, ST PAUL, Minnesota, SEATTLE, Washington, BOSTON, Massachusetts, AUSTIN, Texas and D & S Publishers, CLEARWATER, Florida

British Library Cataloguing in Publication Data

Birts, Peter W.
  Trespass: the summary procedure for
  possession of land.
1. Trespass—England
I. Title   II. Willis, Alan
344.2063'6   KD1966
ISBN 0–406–10481–6

Front cover photograph reproduced by kind permission of The Salisbury Journal.

Typeset by Phoenix Photosetting, Chatham, Kent
Printed in Great Britain by Biddles Ltd, Guildford, Surrey

Foreword

This book deals with a comparatively new and important branch of the law of civil procedure. Conventionally, a sharp distinction is made between the law governing substantive rights and the law governing the procedure for enforcing those rights. But it is well to bear in mind Holmes' observation that 'whenever we trace a leading doctrine of substantive law far enough back, we are very likely to find some forgotten circumstance of procedure at its source' (The Common Law, M De W Howe edn, 1968, 199). And the procedure under Order 113 lies at the very frontier of remedies which can be accommodated in an adversarial system based on principles of natural justice. It is therefore intriguing to speculate what legal historians of the future will say about the impact of this procedure on the development of the substantive rights which it serves to protect.

In the meantime it is necessary to remember the reasons for the creation of this procedure in 1970. The authors of this excellent work point out that its origin is to be found in the 'squatting' problem which has confronted landowners since the 1960s. Rightly, they draw attention to a fact which no one concerned with justice can ignore, namely that, apart from lawless persons who have no respect either for the rights of others or for the criminal law, the pejorative term 'squatters' includes many who are genuinely homeless and others who resort to unlawful occupation of land as a means of sincere social or political protest. On the other hand, it must be recognized that before 1970 the law failed to protect landowners properly: in most cases the landowner's claim was unassailable yet the conventional repossession procedures were slow, cumbersome and expensive. Fair and effective access to justice is the first principle of any civilized system of civil law. Without it private citizens will be tempted to resort to self-help. The procedure under Order 113 was intended to confer a fair and effective remedy to protect existing rights. And successive amendments of the rules improved the new machinery. But in Chapter 4, where the authors discuss the raising of a triable issue by defendants and the approach to be adopted, they rightly caution against too robust an approach. The rules governing summary proceedings for the possession of land must only be used to serve the limited purpose for which they were created.

There is today a mass of material in the form of books and articles, produced by academic lawyers and legal practitioners, on every conceivable branch of the civil law. But civil procedure has always lagged behind. Indeed, English lawyers have traditionally displayed very little interest in civil procedure as a separate subject of legal study in its own right. Since in a sense it deals with form rather than substance it has been neglected. But in reality the attainment of justice is inextricably interwoven with the adequacy of rules of procedure. Fortunately, Sir Jack Jacob's herculean efforts in this field are now beginning to show fruits. To the recent literature in this field Mr Peter Birts and Mr Alan Willis have made a valuable contribution. Their appreciation of the subject has been formed, and refined, in the hard school of litigation. They have produced an admirably clear and accurate statement of the relevant rules.

The authors' manifest aim was to produce an exposition of English law as it is. They have rarely indulged in comments de lege ferenda. That reticence adds interest to their remarks about the practice in the Queen's Bench and Chancery Divisions of the High Court of hearing applications in chambers unless the judge orders otherwise. The authors observe that this practice is a legacy from the days when the jury system held sway in civil cases and that it is an anachronism so far as Order 113 applications are concerned. If the authors' historical explanation for this deviation from the principle that civil proceedings should take place in open court is correct, and if that is nowadays the only justification for it, then their comment is justified. And I know of no explanation for the present practice other than the one suggested by the authors. But perhaps this is part of a somewhat larger problem which merits a separate and critical study.

I unreservedly commend this work to readers.

The Honourable Mr Justice Steyn

Preface

The 'squatters procedure' (as the summary procedure for possession of land is familiarly known) is now used so extensively that it is hard to imagine how landowners managed without it before its introduction in 1970. Particularly as a result of the most recent revision – in which the return date for non-residential land was shortened to two days, the rules for service simplified and jurisdiction given to masters and district registrars to hear cases under it – the procedure is now as rapid and effective as any in the civil armoury providing it is properly used.

This book is aimed at practitioners on two levels. First, it is intended to provide an introduction to the summary procedure for those who, in whatever capacity, come across it for the first time, as often as not in circumstances of urgency, when time for research or for consulting others is short. It is hoped that it will offer them quick and clear guidance on the nature and scope of the procedure and the essential practical steps to be taken under it, whether in the High Court or county court. The procedure has, during its lifetime, acquired something of an aura of technicality which we have tried to dispel.

Above all perhaps, the summary procedure should be intelligible and accessible, and we hope this book will have brought that objective a little closer.

Second, and more ambitiously, it is offered to more experienced practitioners – if nothing else, as a time-saver and source of forms and precedents – and as a respectful reminder that all classes of application for summary possession, even those in the most experienced hands, can occasionally fall victim to procedural mishap and wither and die under the judicial eye.

The book is divided into three parts. Part I traces the origins and development of the procedure (Chapter 1), offers a summary of its main provisions and characteristics (Chapter 2), and contains a detailed analysis of the two aspects of its operation which are considered to be the most important and difficult in practice: the ambit of the procedure (Chapter 3) and the principles to be applied when a defence or triable issue emerges (Chapter 4).

Part II contains a step-by-step, practical guide to the entire procedure, from the preliminary considerations facing every landowner wishing to invoke it (Chapter 5) to the preparation of the necessary evidence and documents (Chapter 6), applications for abridgment of time (Chapter 7) and service of proceedings (Chapter 8), to the hearing itself (Chapter 9). Setting aside of, and appeal against, orders made under the procedure are dealt with in Chapter 10.

Part III is devoted to the important topic of enforcement of an order for possession obtained summarily. Chapter 11 describes the documents essential to the execution process, Chapter 12 gives an account of the duties of the sheriff and the bailiff, while Chapter 13 considers unlawful reoccupation and the (until recently somewhat neglected) remedy of restitution.

It is hoped that the contents of the Appendices will remove the need for the practitioner to look elsewhere: Appendix I contains the relevant Rules of Court; Appendix II a complete collection of the necessary forms and precedents, while Appendix III contains the text of, and comments upon, a less well-known but related summary procedure – that available to local authorities against gipsies under the Caravan Sites Act 1968 Part II.

Although the main thrust of the book is inevitably directed towards the plaintiff who sets the procedure in motion, we have not overlooked the interests of defendants. Both in the text and in Appendix II there will be found guidance for those wishing to defend an application under the summary procedure.

The law is stated as at 1 May 1987.

Many colleagues and friends have helped us with suggestions and encouragement for writing this book and we are grateful to them all. We particularly thank Mr Christopher Jones, Chief Clerk to the Queen's Bench Judge in Chambers and Mr Gordon Sleigh, Sheriff's Officer for the County of Wiltshire, and Mr Frederick Marr-Johnson, Barrister, who each kindly read the manuscript and made a number of valuable comments which we have gratefully incorporated. We also thank the staff of the Chancery Listing Office for their kind help. Last, but by no means least, our admiration and gratitude go to Mrs Anne Lampard who typed the manuscript (in the face of a barrage of last-minute alterations) with a rapidity unmatched by the most expeditious summary possession application.

All this kind help notwithstanding, should there be errors or omissions, we alone must bear responsibility.

Peter Birts
Alan Willis
May 1987

Contents

Chapter 13   Re-occupation by unlawful occupiers: restitution   79

APPENDICES

Appendix I   85

Appendix II   93

Table of statutes

References in this Table to *Statutes* are to Halsbury's Statutes of England (Fourth Edition) showing the volume and page at which the annotated text of the Act may be found. Page references printed in **bold** type indicate where the section of an Act is set out in part or in full.

Table of statutory instruments

Page references printed in **bold** type indicate where a statutory instrument is set out in part or in full.

Table of cases

Part one
The nature and scope of
the summary procedure

Chapter 1

Origins and development

THE EMERGENCE OF THE SUMMARY PROCEDURE

Considering that its precursor, the summary judgment procedure under RSC Order 14, has been an indispensable part of English procedural law for over a century,[1] it is perhaps surprising that the present procedure for the summary recovery of land from trespassers was not available to landowners until 1970, the year in which it was introduced into both the High Court and county court.[2]

Whether this was due to lack of demand for such a procedure or to an out-of-date and misplaced faith in the practicability of self-help as a satisfactory response to trespass to land, or both, the new procedure, once it arrived, was put to extensive use by landowners of all kinds, and soon attracted a modest body of case law to assist in its interpretation and application. The acknowledged success of the procedure over the past 16 years, moreover, has probably helped to create and sustain a jurisprudential climate in which the use

---

1. RSC Order 14 was introduced by the Judicature Act 1875.
2. RSC (Amendment No 2) 1970, (SI 1970/944); County Court (Amendment No 4) Rules 1970, (No 1201 (L26)).

of self-help as a remedy against trespass to land has been firmly discouraged by judges of the highest standing in the civil[3] and criminal[4] fields, and its continued availability as a swift, effective but also just procedure may properly be regarded as an important contribution to the fabric of public order generally, fragile as that sometimes appears.

It is well known that RSC Order 113 and its county court equivalent CCR Order 26 (now CCR 1981, Order 24) were introduced in order to facilitate the speedy removal by civil judicial process not only of those unlawful occupiers of land who could be identified and named by the persons seeking their removal but also, and more importantly, of those who could not.

So far as identification was concerned, it had been decided at first instance in 1969 that since the courts had no power to make a final order against a person who was not a party to an action, a landowner could not proceed by action for an order for possession against unnamed persons.[5] As for named persons, speedy relief from trespass was rarely possible under the existing court procedures, for two reasons. First, the only method of proceeding was by action, in itself a relatively lengthy and cumbersome process, even on a default or undefended basis. Secondly, the Court of Appeal had held that the court had no jurisdiction to make an order for possession of land on an interlocutory (or interim) application.[6] Thus, while the equitable remedy of injunction

---

3. See per Denning MR in *McPhail v Persons (names unknown)* [1973] Ch 447 at 457, [1973] 3 All ER 393 at 396, CA.
4. See per Lawton LJ in *R v Chief Constable of Devon and Cornwall, ex p Central Electricity Generating Board* [1982] QB 458 at 473, [1981] 3 All ER 826 at 834, CA.
5. *Re Wykeham Terrace, Brighton, Sussex, ex p Territorial Auxiliary and Volunteer Reserve Association for the South East* [1971] Ch 204; [1970] 3 WLR 649.
6. *Manchester Corpn v Connolly* [1970] Ch 420, [1970] 1 All ER 961.

was available, as it always had been, in urgent cases to restrain named defendants from entering or remaining on land, the recovery of the land itself by process of execution had to await the final outcome of the action.

These shortcomings in procedural law had been highlighted in the late 1960s when 'squatting' became prevalent both amongst those in society who were genuinely homeless and for that reason had need of empty residential property, and those who, whatever their circumstances, took up occupation of such property for the purpose of making a protest, or gesture of disobedience. Not surprisingly, the reaction of the property owners involved, as well as considerations of public order, rendered the conventional delays in the repossession process unacceptable in such circumstances, whilst the sheer numbers of occupiers (to say nothing of their changing population during the period of occupation) made the task of identifying them a virtually impossible one in most cases.

RSC Order 113 in its original form[7] provided landowners with a wholly new procedure for recovering possession of land from unlawful occupiers which was both expeditious and effective in surmounting the identification problem. It was expeditious in that it provided for a possession order to be made once seven clear days[8] after the date of service of the proceedings on the occupiers had elapsed, and effective in that it allowed an order to be made whoever was occupying the premises at the time of execution of the order, providing the landowner had taken reasonable steps to identify every person occupying them before applying to the court.

---

7. As added by RSC (Amendment No 2) 1970, (SI 1970/944).
8. For the meaning of 'clear days', see below, Chapter 7, page 48.

The 1977 revision

Two important revisions of the procedure were made in 1977.[9] First, the period of seven clear days was reduced to five, it being generally felt that no injustice would be caused to defendants thereby, a judgment which appears to have been a correct one. Secondly, in the light of the difficulties experienced by landowners in proving to the satisfaction of judges (understandably anxious to protect the rights of defendants exposed to a new and special procedure) that reasonable steps had been taken to identify every occupant of the land,[10] this requirement was removed, leaving the present residual obligation on the landowner to name in the summons those occupiers he has identified, and to state that he does not know the name of any person in occupation whom he has not so named.[11]

Other changes brought in at the same time are perhaps of historical interest only, but nevertheless conveniently illustrate the development of the procedure. A requirement was introduced to effect service in the case of land occupied by unnamed defendants by, in addition to affixing a copy of the summons to the main door or other conspicuous part of the premises, inserting it through the letter-box at the premises if practicable. This requirement has been retained but is now, as a result of the 1986 revision, an alternative rather than an obligatory mode of service where unnamed defendants are in occupation.[12]

The fourth and last of the 1977 changes was the placing of a limit of three months on issue without leave of a writ of

---

9. RSC (Amendment No 2) 1977, (SI 1977/960).
10. See *Re 9 Orpen Road, Stoke Newington* [1971] 1 All ER 944; [1971] 1 WLR 166.
11. RSC Order 113, rules 2,3.
12. See below, Chapter 8.

possession under Order 113 – a change intended to discourage landowners from invoking an exceptional and rapid procedure by which to obtain a possession order and then failing to execute it with reasonable promptness.

The 1980 revision

In 1980 a provision was added[13] which confirmed the court's power to order possession to be given on a specified date, in the exercise of any power which could have been exercised if possession had been claimed in an action begun by writ. This provision, which underlines the exclusively procedural nature of the changes brought about by the introduction of Order 113, is an important one to bear in mind when the procedure is being invoked against persons whose original entry to the premises was not without consent; indeed, it is only relevant in such circumstances.[14] Changes corresponding to both the 1977 and the 1980 revisions were made in the county court. Also in 1980 county court registrars were given jurisdiction to make orders under the summary procedure.

The 1986 revision

No sooner had these revisions been promulgated, than a further challenge to the effectiveness of the summary procedure presented itself. Whereas in the first decade or so of its existence the summary procedure was mainly invoked to end unlawful occupations of buildings or land situated in urban areas, the 1980s seemed to herald its more frequent

---

13. RSC (Amendment No 3) 1980, (SI 1980/1908).
14. See below, Chapter 2, pages 11–14.

use against persons such as travellers, caravanners and the like who took up squatting, sometimes in very large numbers, on open rural land.

This pattern of activity came to a head in 1985 with the mass unlawful occupation of parts of the country such as Savernake Forest and Bratton Camp in Wiltshire, followed in 1986 by the occupation of part of the New Forest by members of the so called 'peace convoy'. Public concern was perhaps at its highest when some 300 'hippies' invaded the land of the Somerset farmer, Mr Attwell.

The delays, costs and other difficulties caused to the landowners involved by the need to apply to a judge for directions for service of proceedings on open land, and to abridge the five-day period, in these and other self-evidently urgent but essentially straightforward cases, led to a considerable debate. This involved on the one hand the interests of landowners concerned at the seeming inability of the civil or criminal law to provide a swift remedy to assist those whose land was placed at risk and, on the other, those who argued that existing powers were adequate and that none of the changes being urged was necessary.

In the outcome, the Government added to its by then well-advanced public order legislation a specific police power to require trespassers to leave land under certain circumstances[15] and, at the same time, the Lord Chancellor agreed to re-appraise the operation of the summary procedure.

Wide consultation followed and on 12th January 1987, new rules[16] were introduced into the High Court whereby three further important revisions of the procedure were made.

---

15. See Public Order Act 1986, s 39. For a discussion and analysis of this section see Card, *Public Order—the New Law* (1987).
16. RSC (Amendment No 3) 1986, (SI 1986/2289).

First, the period of five clear days was reduced to two in the case of non-residential premises. Secondly, express provision was made for proceedings to be served in the case of occupation of such land by unnamed defendants by the placing of stakes in the ground at conspicuous parts of the land to which must be affixed a sealed transparent envelope containing a sealed copy of the summons and affidavit. Thirdly, jurisdiction was given to Supreme Court masters (and therefore to district registrars as well)[17] to hear applications under the summary procedure. The five-day period for residential premises was retained in order to allay fears that occupiers in such cases might be placed at a disadvantage in obtaining legal advice were the period to be further shortened in that class of case. Corresponding changes to the County Court Rules were introduced in April 1987.[18]

---

17. See RSC Order 32, rule 3.
18. County Court (Amendment) Rules 1987, SI 1987/493.

Chapter 2

Main features of the summary procedure

THE PROCEDURE IN OUTLINE: A SELF-CONTAINED CODE

RSC Order 113 and CCR 1981, Order 24 provide a summary procedure whereby a person claiming possession of land which he alleges is occupied solely by a person or persons (not being a tenant or tenants holding over after the termination of the tenancy) who entered into or remained in occupation without his licence or consent, or that of any predecessor in title of his, may make application to the court for an order for delivery up of possession. No other relief save costs against named defendants can be claimed in the proceedings. Despite an apparent suggestion to the contrary in the 1985 Supreme Court Practice, the remedy of injunction is not available under Order 113, but must be claimed in an ordinary action for trespass.

The application is made in the High Court by originating summons to which an acknowledgment of service is not required, and in the county court by originating application. With that and certain other exceptions to be mentioned later, the procedures in the High Court and county court are identical. Proceedings in the High Court may be heard and determined by a master or district registrar, who may refer them to a judge if he thinks they should properly be decided by a judge. Proceedings in the county court are heard by the judge and, with the leave of the judge, by the registrar.

Rules of court[1] provide for the form in which the applications are to be made, for the contents of the affidavit evidence to be filed in support and for the manner in which the proceedings are to be served on named occupiers and where unnamed defendants are in occupation of the land. Provision is made for any unnamed person who is in occupation of the land and who wishes to be heard to be joined as a party to the proceedings.

Except in cases of urgency and by leave of the court, an order for possession of residential premises may not be made less than five, and in the case of non-residential premises less than two, clear days after the date of service of the proceedings. The rules prescribe a special form of order for possession[2] to be used in all cases and empower the court to specify a date for possession to be given in cases where it would have had such a power had the proceedings been begun by action.[3]

An important feature is that, unlike ordinary actions in the High Court for possession of land,[4] no leave is required to issue a writ of possession, providing such writ is issued within three months of the date of the order. An application for such leave may, unless the court directs otherwise, be

---

1. RSC Order 113, rules 1–8; CCR 1981 Order 24, rules 1–7 set out in full below, pages 85–91.
2. Form No 42A (High Court); Form N36 (county court) see below, pages 95, 99.
3. See below, page 14.
4. Which are governed by RSC Order 45, rule 3.

made ex parte. The writ or, in the county court, warrant of possession must also be in a special prescribed form.[5] Finally, the court is given express power to set aside or vary an order for possession on such terms as it thinks just.

It will be appreciated from the above that the rules in both the High Court and the county court provide, in effect, a unique and self-contained code of procedure which is to be followed by those wishing to take advantage of its exceptional provisions.

IMPORTANT GENERAL CHARACTERISTICS

The code has the following important general characteristics which should be borne in mind throughout by those concerned in its proper operation.

First, it is a *purely procedural* code which makes no alteration to the substantive law of possession against trespassers, or to the extent or nature of the court's jurisdiction to grant orders for possession of land.[6] Thus wherever the plaintiff would be entitled to an order for possession were he to proceed by action he will, providing he complies with the code's provisions, be entitled to obtain such an order summarily.[7]

Secondly, because of its exceptional and summary nature, its *provisions must be strictly construed* and orders for possession

---

5. Form No 66A (High Court); Form N52 (county court) see below, pages 96, 100.
6. *University of Essex v Djemal* [1980] 2 All ER 742; [1980] 1 WLR 1301, CA.
7. *Wiltshire County Council v Frazer* (1983) 82 LGR 313; 47 P & CR 69, CA.

under it not made unless its requirements are strictly and fully complied with.[8] Thirdly, it must be *properly invoked* and not abused. Again, because of its summary nature, it has been said that it must not be used by a landowner when there is an arguable defence,[9] or where a highly complicated question of title is in issue.[10] However, whether to invoke the procedure in the first place or to continue with an application made under it if a triable issue emerges at any stage in the proceedings is sometimes not an easy decision for practitioners to make, nor is it always a simple matter for the court to decide whether to hear an application in which a triable issue is raised or whether to adjourn it. Analogies with RSC Order 14 can be helpful, providing they are not carried too far.

The summary procedure for possession is, moreover, to be distinguished from the summary judgment procedure in this important respect: whereas a plaintiff is not entitled to proceed at all under Order 14 if there is a defence to the claim or triable issue likely to be raised (indeed, he must file an affidavit deposing to his belief that there is no defence), under Order 113 (and CCR 1981, Order 24) not only is there no requirement for such an affidavit, but the procedure specifically contemplates or accommodates a trial of sorts with the defendant, if he attends, being invited to be heard.

---

8. Ibid, (1983) 82 LGR 313 at p 316; 47 P & CR 69 at 72. Providing no injustice will be caused, the court has a discretion to waive any irregularity of the summary procedure under RSC Order 2 rule 1: see per Oliver J in *Burston Finance Ltd v Wilkins & Persons Unknown*, (1975) Times, 17 July. In practice, however, the court is slow to assist a plaintiff who has failed fully to comply with the procedure by exercising its discretion under this rule.

9. *Southwark London Borough Council v Williams* [1971] Ch 734, [1971] 2 All ER 175, CA.

10. *Cudworth v Masefield* (1984) Times, 15 May.

Far from there being no issue and no trial, therefore, as under Order 14, there may very well be an issue raised under Order 113 which is triable. But the procedure, assuming it has been properly invoked, will only be continued if the issue is one which can be *tried summarily*. This topic, which goes to the heart of the effectiveness of the summary procedure, is considered in greater detail in Chapter 4, where what are perceived to be the relevant principles are set out.

Fourthly, where the court is satisfied that its provisions have been strictly complied with as a matter of construction and that the procedure has been properly invoked, the *court has no discretion* to prevent a plaintiff from using it,[11] or to refuse him possession even if he is not using it for the purpose of overcoming one of the shortcomings of less summary procedures by reason of which it was introduced,[12] or to suspend an order for possession against persons who have entered and remained as trespassers unless the owner consents, either in the High Court[13] or county court.[14] As has already been noted, the court can specify a date for possession, but only in those cases where it would have had that power had the proceedings been brought by action, ie not in relation to persons who entered and remained as trespassers but in relation, for example, to former licensees such as service

---

11. *Greater London Council v Jenkins* [1975] 1 All ER 354; [1975] 1 WLR 155, CA. Cf *West Glamorgan County Council v Rafferty* [1987] 1 All ER 1005, [1987] 1 WLR 457, CA, where a local authority's decision to evict gipsies was held void for unreasonableness having regard to its duty to provide accommodation under the Caravan Sites Act 1968, s 6(1), ie as a matter of substantive law.
12. *Wiltshire County Council v Frazer* (1983) 82 LGR 313 at 320, 47 P & CR 69 at 76.
13. *McPhail v Persons (names unknown)* [1973] Ch 447, [1973] 3 All ER 393, CA.
14. *Swordheath Properties Ltd v Floyd* [1978] 1 All ER 721; [1978] 1 WLR 550, CA.

occupants whose licences have been lawfully revoked so as to make them amenable to the procedure.[15]

The next chapter will examine the requirements that must be met by a landowner wishing to bring himself within the ambit of the procedure.

---

15. See below, Chapter 3. For the restrictions on the discretion of the court in making orders for possession of land in such cases, see Housing Act 1980, s 89.

Chapter 3
Ambit

In view of the strict construction placed by the court on the terms of the summary procedure, it is necessary to examine the wording of rule 1 of RSC Order 113 and CCR 1981, Order 24 carefully in order to determine the circumstances which must be present for a landowner to bring himself within its ambit. The wording of Order 113 is identical to that of Order 24 for present purposes, so it will be convenient to begin by setting out Order 113, rule 1 which provides as follows:

> 'Where a person claims possession of land which he alleges is occupied solely by a person or persons (not being a tenant or tenants holding over after the termination of the tenancy) who entered into or remained in occupation without his licence or consent or that of any predecessor in title of his, the proceedings may be brought by originating summons in accordance with the provisions of this Order.'

In other words, if a person wants to claim possession of land from a trespasser in the particular circumstances set out in the rule, then he may proceed to do so by originating summons in accordance with the provisions of the Order, ie rules 2–8 inclusive.

Part II of this book contains a detailed discussion of rules 2–8 (and their county court equivalent) and offers guidance on the essentially practical task of complying with them. In this chapter we shall seek to identify and delineate the particular circumstances set out in rule 1. In the High Court the parties to an application are called respectively 'the plaintiff' and 'the defendant' and in the county court 'the applicant' and 'the respondent'. For brevity, we shall now refer to 'the plaintiff and 'the defendant'.

THE THREE REQUIREMENTS

Rule 1 contains essentially three requirements, each of which must be met if a plaintiff is to bring himself within the ambit of the Order. They are:
1. That the plaintiff should be a person claiming possession of land;
2. That the land should be occupied solely by a person who entered into or remained in occupation without the licence or consent of the plaintiff or his predecessor in title;
3. That the defendant should not be a tenant holding over after the termination of the tenancy.
Each of these calls for further elaboration.

The first requirement

'That the plaintiff should be a person claiming possession of land'.

Person

The word 'person' includes not only a human person but

also a body of persons corporate or unincorporate.[1] Thus, for example, a club, limited company, local authority or government department can avail itself of the Order.

Possession

Although the rule makes no mention of an entitlement to possession, the word 'claims' presupposes that the plaintiff must, in order to bring himself within the rule, be the person entitled to possession of the land claimed. This is merely a procedural reflection of the substantive law, it being axiomatic that the only person who can bring an action for trespass is the person in possession, or with an immediate right to possession of the land as against the trespasser,[2] but it is one that should never be lost sight of. 'Possession' is a difficult concept in law but for present purposes it simply means control and enjoyment of the land in question. Thus the person who is controlling and enjoying it (or entitled to be enjoying it) is the person entitled to its possession.

Possession must be distinguished sharply from *ownership* which is a concept of title. If an owner of land does not let or licence it to another for that other's use or enjoyment, then clearly he retains both ownership and possession of the land. If, however, he grants a lease or tenancy of it, the lessee or tenant will enjoy possession as against his landlord, the owner, and will be entitled to exclude him from possession just as he would a complete stranger such as a squatter. Possession is a relative rather than an absolute concept. To support a claim for possession against a trespasser, a plaintiff need only assert possession and his intention to regain it.

---

1. Interpretation Act 1978, Sch 1.
2. 45 *Halsbury's Laws* (4th edn), para 1396.

It will then be for the defendant to set up some right to possession which is better than the plaintiff's.[3]

It follows that it is the person entitled to possession who is the appropriate plaintiff to bring summary proceedings for possession of land, just as that person is the appropriate plaintiff in an action for trespass, a cause of action usually defined as an unjustifiable interference with the possession of land.

It is surprising how often difficulties are encountered in practice in correctly identifying the person or persons entitled to possession. These are difficulties of substantive law which are beyond the scope of this book. However, it is essential to be aware of them when use of the summary procedure is being considered and some of them are discussed in Chapter 5.

Land

'Land' has the meaning usually given to it under the law and therefore includes buildings and other structures, land covered with water and any estate, interest, easement, servitude or right in or over land.[4]

It includes the surface of the highway, the owner in fee simple determinable of which is entitled to use the summary procedure against persons who occupy it by blocking it even though not so as to obstruct it completely.[5] Moreover, the

---

3. *Delaney v T P Smith Ltd* [1946] KB 393, [1946] 2 All ER 23; see also *Portland Managements Ltd v Harte* [1977] QB 306, [1976] 1 All ER 225.
4. Interpretation Act 1978, Sch 1.
5. *Wiltshire County Council v Frazer* (1983) 82 LGR 313, 47 P & CR 69, CA.

court's jurisdiction to make a summary possession order of land, not all of which is unlawfully occupied, is not limited to that area of land which is in unlawful occupation, since the court has jurisdiction to protect the right of the owner to possession of the whole of his property, uninterfered with by unauthorised adverse possession. However, the extent of the field of operation of such an order will depend on the circumstances of the case.[6]

The second requirement

'That the land should be occupied solely by a person who has entered into or remained in occupation without the licence or consent of the plaintiff or his predecessor in title'.

Occupied

Occupation in the context of this rule is a much lesser concept than possession. It means, in effect, any physical presence on the land or any part of the land constituting an interference with possession which is of sufficient significance and permanence to justify the use of the procedure by the plaintiff. Unlike the concept of possession, there is seldom any difficulty in practice in recognising whether a person is or is not in occupation.

Solely

The inclusion of the word 'solely' in the rule brings about a qualification of the ambit of the procedure which is more

---

6. *University of Essex v Djemal* [1980] 2 All ER 742; [1980] 1 WLR 1301, CA; and see pages 37–38, below.

considerable than is perhaps widely realised. It means that if an unlawful occupier of land is not the sole occupier (for example, if he shares occupation with another person such as a licensee of the plaintiff or any other person who is not a defendant to the proceedings) the procedure cannot be invoked against him. This may at first sight seem to be a serious disadvantage to landowners. However, when it is remembered that an order for possession of land, once obtained, is enforceable by writ or warrant of possession[7] and, if necessary, of restitution[8] against all persons found on the premises at the time of execution whether they were parties to the original proceedings or not, it will be appreciated that the inclusion of the word 'solely' constitutes an important safeguard for lawful occupiers.

For this reason it is necessary for the court to have before it evidence from which it can be satisfied that the land is occupied solely by the defendant or defendants before making an order for possession: it is not a matter which the court should be expected to infer. This may be particularly important where large areas of land or buildings in multi-occupancy are involved.

Person

Since the word 'person' includes a body of persons corporate it is theoretically possible for an entity such as a limited company to be amenable to the procedure through its servants or agents, although such cases are likely to be rare.

---

7. *R v Wandsworth County Court, ex p London Borough of Wandsworth* [1975] 3 All ER 390; [1975] 1 WLR 1314.

8. Providing there is a sufficient nexus between the circumstances of the original occupation and the subsequent re-occupation; *Wiltshire County Council v Frazer (No 2)* [1986] 1 All ER 65, [1986] 1 WLR 109.

Entered into or remained in occupation without licence or consent

The inclusion of the words 'or remained' makes it clear that the procedure can be used against persons whose original entry into occupation was with consent but who have remained in occupation after the determination or revocation of their licence, ie to licensees holding over.[9] As has already been seen, the court has no discretion to withhold the use of the procedure in these circumstances even if, as seems plain, the rule was not introduced with such persons in mind. In consequence, although judges and writers have in the past expressed disquiet about its use in such circumstances, service, holiday and other occupants such as licensees with a restricted contract under s 106A of the Rent Act 1977, and licensees under rental purchase agreements governed by s 88 of the Housing Act 1980 are as a matter of construction within the ambit of the order. If, however, a triable issue is raised at any stage as to the lawful termination of the relevant licence, the court is likely to be unsympathetic to the continued use of the procedure. The question whether a licence has been lawfully determined *vis à vis* a particular defendant or defendants may require careful consideration where the land concerned is land to which the public has access, for example, land used for recreational purposes, local authority gipsy sites and land surrounding ancient monuments. In these cases, reference must be made to the legislation giving rise to the relevant licence and two questions asked; (a) was the plaintiff empowered to determine the defendant's licence;[10] and (b) if so, was the manner of determination reasonable in law.

---

9. *Greater London Council v Jenkins* [1975] 1 All ER 354, [1975] 1 WLR 155, CA.

10. The defendant may be a trespasser ab initio if he has so conducted himself as to have exceeded the terms of any licence: see 45 *Halsbury's Laws* (4th edn), para 1389.

The plaintiff or his predecessor in title

If the plaintiff's precedessor in title has granted a licence to the occupier to occupy the land, such licence must have been lawfully determined by the plaintiff before the case can come within the ambit of the procedure.

The third requirement

'That the defendant should not be a tenant holding over after the termination of the tenancy'.

The third requirement which must be complied with is that the defendant should not be a tenant holding over after the termination of the tenancy. Whether or not an occupier has what amounts to a tenancy can, of course, sometimes be a very difficult matter to determine.[11] All that need be noticed here, however, is that if a defendant appears to have a colourable claim to be a tenant the court may not permit the summary procedure to be used against him.[12] It has been held at first instance[13] that the procedure can be used by a landlord against an illegal subtenant, on the ground that the tenancy referred to in the rule means a tenancy binding on the person claiming possession, which a subtenancy granted in breach of an absolute prohibition against subletting and without the knowledge of the plaintiff would not be. However, there would seem to be nothing in the wording of the rule to warrant this interpretation, the correctness of which, it is submitted, is open to doubt on a variety of

---

11. See *Street v Mountford* [1985] AC 809, [1985] 2 All ER 289 HL.
12. See below, Chapter 4.
13. *Moore Properties (Ilford) Ltd v McKeon* [1977] 1 All ER 262; [1976] 1 WLR 1278.

grounds. Even if the decision is correct, the fact that the point is an important one deserving of full argument were the decision to be questioned means that an application by a landowner against an illegal subtenant under the summary procedure might be an incautious use of the procedure.[14]

Once it has been determined whether the requirements of rule 1 are met or likely to be met as a matter of construction, it is necessary to consider whether a triable issue or arguable defence has been or is likely to be raised and, if so, whether the plaintiff may be prevented from invoking the summary procedure, or from pursuing an application already made under it. This is discussed in the next chapter.

---

14. See below, Chapter 4.

Chapter 4

The raising of a triable issue

Although most of the reported cases under the summary procedure are concerned with matters of ambit and jurisdiction, it is more common than is sometimes supposed for problems to arise in practice because a triable issue or arguable defence is raised to the plaintiff's claim either by the defendant, if he opposes the application, or by the court itself whether or not the application is opposed.

Apart from the unfortunate fact that, as we have seen, the question of ambit can generate its own crop of arguments, a combination of procedural strictness and judicial vigilance to protect the interests of the defendant can lead to the dilemma of whether, an issue having been raised, it is appropriate to embark on or continue with a summary hearing at all. The dilemma is not a new one, because under RSC Order 14 the courts have long been used to deciding whether a defendant has by affidavit evidence succeeded in raising a triable issue such as will entitle him to leave to defend. However, the dilemma is often more acute under the summary procedure for possession of land for a variety of reasons. In the first place the defendant's home (rather than his money) is usually at stake and the application for possession is almost invariably urgent from the plaintiff's point of view. It is also the case that, even with the recent revisions,

RSC Order 113 is still a good deal more technical in its operation than Order 14 has ever been. Lastly, the substantive defences that can be raised in answer to a claim for possession of land tend to be more complex (or more unfamiliar to the majority of practitioners) than those usually encountered in applications under Order 14 and are generally raised orally, unsupported by affidavit evidence and without prior warning to the plaintiff or his adviser.

THE APPROACH OF THE COURT

The approach adopted by the court towards the use of the summary procedure when a triable issue arises has become more flexible in recent years and, it is submitted, more legally correct. In *Southwark London Borough Council v Williams*[1] Lord Denning MR took the robust view that the procedure should be used 'only where there is no arguable defence.' A few years later, however, in *Shah v Givert*[2] the Court of Appeal held that the procedure may be used if there is a triable issue, providing on the evidence the matter is 'clear and straightforward', Bridge LJ observing that there was nothing in Order 113 or CCR Order 26 (now CCR 1981, Order 24) which disentitled the court in summary proceedings for possession of land from trying an issue which emerged in the proceedings. Eventually, in *Henderson v Law*,[3] Griffiths LJ, in a judgment concurred in by Sir John Donaldson MR, clarified the position to a great extent by holding that, at least in cases where an issue arises as to whether a tenancy or holding over existed, the court has a discretion as to how to proceed, to be exercised in the following manner:

---

1. [1971] Ch 734 at 740, [1971] 2 All ER 175 at 177, CA.
2. (1980) 124 Sol Jo 513, CA.
3. (1984) 17 HLR 237.

1. If it was apparent to the plaintiff that a serious issue was bound to arise as to whether a tenancy or holding over existed, the court would no doubt regard the use of the summary procedure as inappropriate or even, in an extreme case, as an abuse of the process, and dismiss the application;
2. If, however, such an issue arises which, from the plaintiff's point of view, is unexpected, then the court must decide whether in its discretion to continue the summary hearing, to adjourn it for a further (summary) hearing after the parties have had a chance to reconsider the position, or whether the application should be dismissed and the applicant left to have the issues determined in a subsequent action;[4]
3. The mere assertion by a defendant, without warning, that there is either a tenancy or holding over, cannot of itself be a sufficient reason for saying that the use of the summary procedure was inappropriate.

It is submitted that this approach should be followed in all cases where a triable issue is expected or raised, at every stage of the proceedings, and that the court's discretion should not be fettered by semantic or legalistic considerations as to whether a particular issue is serious, triable or arguable, those adjectives being interchangeable so far as RSC Order 113 is concerned. It will be for the court to say

---

4. Further options in the High Court are:
   (i) to give directions under RSC Order 28, rule 4(3) as to how further proceedings on the summons should be heard: see *Islamic Republic of Pakistan v Ghani* (1977) 121 Sol Jo 86, CA;
   (ii) to direct that the proceedings be continued as if begun by writ under RSC Order 28, rule 8; and
   (iii) having so directed, to order that the matter be transferred to the county court, under the County Courts Act 1984, s 40.

   In practice, this last course is the most usually followed, and it is rare for an application to be dismissed if an issue has arisen unexpectedly. In the county court too, the matter can be directed to proceed as an ordinary action. See County Courts Act 1984, s 76.

whether any particular issue that arises is triable and, if so, when and how it should be tried. Providing it has satisfied itself that the defendant has had sufficient time to prepare his case, the court will not hesitate to embark on a lengthy summary determination of a wealth of issues, both factual and legal, if the urgency and importance of the occasion demands, since the word 'summary' does not refer to the length of the hearing.[5] And where the court feels able to consider a point of law or construction of a document without reference to contested facts, then, it is submitted, it will follow the now-settled practice in applications under RSC Order 14 and—

'. . . see whether there is any substance in the proposed defence. If it concludes that, although arguable, the point is bad, then it will give judgment for the plaintiffs . . . But if the court concludes that the plaintiffs are not entitled to judgment because the case raises problems which should be argued and considered fully, then it will give leave to defend'.[6]

Thus, where a defendant puts forward at a summary possession hearing sufficient material to disclose that a licence agreement is arguably a sham in the sense that issues are raised which cannot be resolved without the process of trial and cross examination, the plaintiff's claim will not be sufficiently clear and straightforward for a possession order to be made summarily, and the case will be remitted for trial.[7]

---

5. Per Hutchison J in *Ministry of Defence v Rawle* (26 June 1985, unreported) QB, a mass trespass case heard over three days.
6. Per Kerr LJ in *Sethia (SL) Liners Ltd v State Trading Corpn of India Ltd* [1985] 1 WLR 1398, at 1401, CA.
7. *Markou v Da Silvaesa; Crancour v Merola* (1986) 52 P & CR 204, CA following *Shah v Givert* and *Henderson v Law* above.

REVIEW OF THE COURT'S DISCRETION BY THE COURT OF APPEAL

As to the review of the court's discretion by the Court of Appeal, there would seem to be no valid reason for the Order 14 practice not to be applicable, namely that a discretion as to the existence of a triable issue of law will be reviewable,[8] whereas a discretion as to the existence of evidence and fact is one with which the Court of Appeal will be most unlikely to interfere.[9]

---

8. *European Asian Bank AG v Punjab and Sind Bank* [1983] 2 All ER 508; [1983] 1 WLR 642, CA.
9. *Lloyds Bank Plc v Ellis-Fewster* [1983] 2 All ER 424; [1983] 1 WLR 559, CA.

Part two
Invoking the
summary procedure

Chapter 5

Preliminary considerations

Swift and effective operation of the summary procedure depends in practice upon a combination of factors. The application must be properly constituted, that is, the correct parties must be joined and the appropriate premises or area of land intended to be protected by a possession order clearly delineated. The application must be within the ambit of the procedure, so as to give the court jurisdiction to make an order in a summary manner. The procedure must be strictly and fully complied with so far as its own self-contained code is concerned and it must be properly invoked in the sense discussed in the last chapter. Correct decisions must be made at an early stage as to the need either for an application to abridge the time between service of the proceedings and the hearing in a really urgent case, or for an application for directions as to service before the main hearing. Finally, the most suitable venue for the application must be chosen, that is the county court or High Court, and if the High Court, the Queen's Bench Division or the Chancery Division. The right decisions on these points are essential if the application is to be placed on a sound footing.

A SUGGESTED APPROACH

A suggested approach to these important considerations is
for a landowner intending to invoke the procedure to satisfy
himself about the following matters at the outset:
1. Who the correct plaintiff should be;
2. Who the correct defendant should be;
3. What premises or area of land should be included in the
   application;
4. Whether the proposed application is within the ambit of
   the summary procedure;
5. Whether any defence or triable issue is expected to be
   raised by or on behalf of any defendant;
6. What is the most appropriate venue for the application.
These questions will be addressed in this chapter. The practical steps involved in complying with the rules will be dealt
with in the remainder of Part Two.

The correct plaintiff

As has already been noted[1] the appropriate plaintiff in an
application under the summary procedure is the person who
would be the appropriate plaintiff in an action for trespass. If
the owner has not let or parted with possession of the
premises he will obviously be the plaintiff. If, however, the
land has been let, so as to give rise to an ordinary landlord
and tenant situation, the tenant will be the plaintiff rather
than the landlord, just as where an exclusive licence has
been granted, the licensee not the licensor will bring the
proceedings. Difficulties arise in practice in three main
classes of case:
1. In landlord and tenant situations, where the subsistence

---

1. See above, Chapter 3.

of the tenancy is in question, for example, following service of a notice to quit or forfeiture proceedings, the effect or validity of which is in doubt,[2] following the tenant's death intestate[3] or as a result of his absence from the premises so as to give rise to an inference of surrender;[4]

2. In licence situations, where the subsistence of the licence is in question, or where the possession transferred by the licence is unclear, for example, where a lodger has occupation of rooms not amounting to exclusive possession or tenancy, in which case the house owner will generally be the plaintiff; or where a grazing licence or licence to extract minerals is granted over the land, when it will be a matter of construction of the agreement as to who has been dispossessed by a trespasser;

3. In cases where the land is in the ownership or control of statutory bodies and the incidence of the immediate possessory interest is not readily apparent. Examples of this are land owned by the Ministry of Agriculture for management by the Forestry Commission, the statute providing that the Minister retains the right to let or grant any interest or right over the land;[5] highways becoming trunk roads owned by the Department of Transport for maintenance by local highway authorities,[6] where the Department generally retains possession; land vested in the Department of the Environment for occupation and management by the Historic Buildings and Monuments Commission[7] where, however, possession is vested in the

2. *City of Westminster Assurance Co Ltd v Ainis* (1975) 119 Sol Jo 135, 29 P & CR 469.
3. *Wirral Borough Council v Smith* [1982] 80 LGR 628, CA (1982) 43 P & CR 312.
4. *Preston Borough Council v Fairclough* (1982) Times 15 December, 8 HLR 70, CA; *Henderson v Law* (1984) 17 HLR 237.
5. Forestry Act 1967, s 39(3).
6. Highways Act 1980, s 265.
7. National Heritage Act 1983, ss 33,34.

Commission; and land subject to an access agreement made between a planning authority and a landowner, for the purpose of open air recreation.[8] In cases such as these it is necessary to consult the relevant statutory provisions to determine where the possessory interest lies.

If it is not possible to resolve a doubt as to which of two persons should be the correct plaintiff it may be possible to join both, providing there is no conflict of interest and each consents[9] and providing they are between them indisputably entitled to possession. If these criteria are absent, however, the use of the summary procedure will almost certainly be inappropriate.

The correct defendant

So far as joining the correct defendant is concerned, the requirement is for the plaintiff to name in the summons those occupiers whom he has identified and to state in his affidavit in support that he does not know the name of any person occupying the land who is not so named.[10] It should be emphasised that there is no longer any requirement to take reasonable steps to identify the occupiers, although such identification may result from the making of the usual enquiries and observations that are necessary for the preparation of evidence and, if established, must be deposed to.[11] Every person in unlawful occupation should be joined as a defendant by name, where this is known, or where it is not, under the style of 'person(s) unknown'. As noted above,[12] the

---

8. National Parks and Access to the Countryside Act 1949, s 64.
9. See RSC Order 15, rule 6(2) and CCR 1981 Order 5, rule 2.
10. RSC Order 113, rules 2, 3; CCR 1981, Order 24, rules 2,3.
11. See below, Chapter 6.
12. See above, Chapter 3, pages 20–21.

procedure cannot be used where occupation is shared between lawful and unlawful occupiers.

The appropriate premises or area of land

In cases involving dwellings or medium size buildings, selection of the premises to be included in the application will not ordinarily cause difficulty. Where, however, large buildings or estates of land only part of which is unlawfully occupied are concerned, it is necessary first to determine the precise area which is in unlawful occupation, and secondly, to decide whether only that part requires the protection of an order, or whether some other part or indeed the whole of the premises or parcel of land affected should be included so as to prevent the defendants from moving to the unoccupied part as soon as a possession order is enforced. As already noted, the court has jurisdiction to protect the right of the owner to possession of the whole of his property even though only part is in unlawful occupation, but the extent of the field of operation of such an order will depend on the circumstances.[13] This means that a court being asked to make an order over a wide area of unaffected land must be furnished with the necessary evidence before it will be persuaded to do so.[14]

It will obviously be of advantage to owners of large buildings or estates of land to protect as much of their property as possible by means of an order for possession, particularly since any later, fresh occupation of the land may be dealt with by the even more summary process of writ or warrant of

---

13. See above, Chapter 3, page 20 and *University of Essex v Djemal* [1980] 2 All ER 742, [1980] 1 WLR 1301, CA.
14. See below, Chapter 6.

restitution.[15] However, given the strictness of the summary procedure and the clear possibility of abuse, the courts are likely to ensure that the *University of Essex* principle is kept firmly within proper bounds.

Ambit

The application having been constituted, the next step is to ensure that all the circumstances are present which are necessary to bring it within the ambit of the procedure as analysed in Chapter 3 above. It is suggested that at this point a plaintiff should satisfy himself that the three requirements there referred to are likely to be met in his case.

Triable issue or defence

Next it is necessary to ask whether any defence to the application is likely to be raised or argued and, if so, what. As explained in Chapter 4, if a defence of substance or difficulty is expected, it will generally be unwise to pursue an application under the procedure, since the application may in these circumstances be held to be an abuse.[16] On the other hand, if an argument is anticipated which the plaintiff genuinely and confidently considers to be bad, and likely to be rejected by the court at a summary hearing, he will be justified in using the procedure, although he will probably be wise to disclose the existence of the anticipated argument and his answer to it in his affidavit, in order to demonstrate that the application is made in good faith.

---

15. See *Wiltshire County Council v Frazer (No 2)* [1986] 1 All ER 65, [1986] 1 WLR 109 and below, Chapter 13.
16. See above Chapter 4, pages 27–28.

It should be remarked here that the question of whether a triable issue or defence is likely to arise, although logically presenting itself at this point for initial consideration, should be kept under review throughout the proceedings.

Choice of venue

The main choice is between the High Court and the county court. If the High Court is chosen, proceedings may be begun in the Queen's Bench Division or Chancery Division, either in London or a district registry. Since the 1986 rules revision, moreover, masters and district registrars have been given the jurisdiction to hear summary possession applications which were previously heard only by judges. The factors to be considered in making the choice are:
1. jurisdiction
2. procedural factors
3. difficulty of law
4. enforcement
5. cost.

(i) *Jurisdiction*

Since the summary procedure is purely procedural in character, the limit of the court's jurisdiction is that applicable to actions for possession of land, that is, the county court has jurisdiction providing the rateable value of the land does not exceed £1,000.[17] Where the land is unrated, as with much open land, this will not be a relevant factor.

---

17. County Courts Act 1984, s 21. As to the county court limit of jurisdiction see Administration of Justice Act 1973, s 6, Sch 2.

(ii) *Procedural factors*

Important procedural factors to be considered are the location and availability of a judge, master or registrar (including a district registrar) as well as other necessary court officers, and the matter of publicity. In the county court the hearing is in open court, whereas in the High Court it is in chambers, unless adjourned into open court.[18] Other factors are the difference in the reckoning of the time between service and the return date and the mode of applying for abridgment of time.[19] Where a speedy hearing is required, and whether or not abridgment of time is necessary, inquiries of the listing officers in the Queen's Bench and Chancery Divisions and in the local county court, will elicit which venue can offer the earliest return date.[20]

(iii) *Difficulty of law*

As has already been noted, difficulties of law do sometimes occur in the course of applications for summary possession. Not the least of these is the question of whether a particular issue or defence is triable or not – something which may be difficult to determine and which may itself be partly a question of law. Notwithstanding the experience of the county court in property law generally, issues occasionally arise which are of sufficient difficulty or importance to merit a hearing in the High Court. In this event, further choices have to be made between the Queen's Bench and the Chancery Divisions and between a judge and a master. Those choices will be made by practitioners on conventional grounds, but it is not expected that judges of the High Court will be asked to hear very many applications under the summary procedure as a result of the 1986 revision.

---

18. RSC Order 32, rules 13,18. And see below, Chapter 9.
19. See below, Chapter 7.
20. No court or Division has a monopoly of speed: the availability of judges, masters and registrars to hear urgent cases varies from court to court and from day to day.

(iv) *Enforcement*

The principal difference between the execution process in the county court and that in the High Court is that whereas in the former it is carried out by warrant addressed to the bailiff, in the latter it is effected by means of writ addressed to the sheriff. Both officers may have need to call on outside agencies including the police in order to complete their duties, and it may be that practitioners have in the past entertained assumptions as to the relative effectiveness of the parallel procedures which are not borne out by experience. Partly for this reason, the subject of enforcement is dealt with in some detail in Part Three of this book.[21]

(v) *Cost*

In the High Court the fees are:

On the issue of the originating summons	£60
On the issue of the praecipe for the writ of possession	£6

The fee payable to the sheriff is discussed in Chapter 12.

At the time of writing the fees payable in the county court for a summary possession application are as follows:

On the issue of the originating application	£43
On the issue of the warrant of possession	£25

No separate fee is payable to the bailiff.

---

21. See below, Chapter 12.

Chapter 6

The preparation of evidence and documents

ORIGINATING PROCESS

In the High Court

The action is commenced by the use of the form of Originating Summons prescribed in Form 11A in Appendix A to the RSC. This form is reproduced in Appendix II to this book.[1]

In the county court

The application is by way of Originating Application in form N312 of the County Court Forms. This form is also reproduced in Appendix II to this book.[2]

AFFIDAVIT IN SUPPORT

Note: For present purposes RSC Order 113, rule 3 is identical to CCR 1981, Order 24, rule 2. In this chapter, except

---

1. See below, page 94.
2. See below, page 98.

where specifically noted, all references are to the High Court procedure.

The requirements of the rule

RSC Order 113, rule 3 provides:

> The plaintiff shall file in support of the originating summons an affidavit stating—
> (a) his interest in the land;
> (b) the circumstances in which the land has been occupied without licence or consent and in which his claim to possession arises;
>   and
> (c) that he does not know the name of any person occupying the land who is not named in the summons.

Since in practice the Court rarely hears oral evidence in support of an application under this procedure, the accurate and careful drafting of this document is of the utmost importance if the application is to succeed fully. It is therefore proposed to examine the requirements of the rule in detail. Suggested forms of affidavit are to be found in Appendix II.[3]

Preliminary

First it should be noted that the plaintiff himself may not necessarily be the deponent. If this is the case, care should be taken to ensure that any necessary written authority, resolu-

---

3. See below, pages 104–109.

tion, etc. either to authorise the proceedings themselves, or to give a person authority to depose on behalf of the plaintiff is clearly set out and, if appropriate, exhibited.

His interest in the land

We have already examined in some detail the principles governing the choice of the plaintiff or plaintiffs.[4] Since the basis of the proceedings is entitlement to possession, that entitlement should be specifically asserted and fully supported.

The rule does not require the plaintiff to prove his entitlement to possession by reference to his ownership. If, however, such proof is readily available, it should be referred to in the affidavit and the deponent should state that the documents, or copies of them, will be available at the hearing. Production of the relevant documents at the hearing will in most cases answer any point taken by a defendant on the plaintiff's right to possession.

Identification of the land

This should present no problem in residential cases. A simple reference to the postal address of the property is sufficient. In cases where, for example, a flat forming part of a larger property is alleged to be unlawfully occupied, care should be taken to ensure that the court and, more particularly, the sheriff or bailiff, can readily identify it so that no person is evicted from a part of the property not within the order for possession.

---

4. See above, Chapter 3 and Chapter 5.

Problems of identification may arise where large areas of land are involved. In this type of case, a plan is virtually indispensable. It should be as small as possible, consistent with clarity: unwieldy plans are not welcomed on the Bench. In cases where a number of plaintiffs with different possessory interests jointly bring proceedings, their respective holdings should be clearly differentiated. Ideally, this should be done by reference to different colours. Where, however, a large number of copies are required in circumstances of urgency, the preparation of a coloured plan may be irksome and a system of black edging, hatching and cross-hatching readily reproducible on a photocopier may be more convenient.

The circumstances in which the land has been occupied without licence or consent and in which his claim to possession arises

The contents of this part of the affidavit will depend entirely on the particular circumstances of the alleged trespass.

The following points should be borne in mind.

Termination of any licence or consent previously given   Particulars should be given of any permission that may have previously been given to the defendants to enter the premises and of the circumstances under which that permission has come to an end, or been determined. Arguments of law, which are for the hearing, should not be set out, but sufficient facts should be given to ensure that the application, on its face, comes within the ambit of the procedure.[5]

Public rights   A statement commonly made by defendants in

---

5. See above, Chapter 3.

non-residential cases is that they are on the premises in exercise of some, usually unspecified, public right. The deponent should detail any rights over the land exercisable by the public and point out, if this be the case, why these are in his view immaterial to any issue in the proceedings. In cases where the land is subject to a statutory right of access, the affidavit should give particulars of the manner in which that right has been determined so far as the defendant is concerned. Where trespass ab initio is relied on, particulars of damage to the premises should be included.[6]

Acquiescence   If the occupation has lasted for any significant period, allegedly without licence or consent, the reasons for this should be particularised. It is frequently asserted by defendants that they have been encouraged to stay and that they have received facilities from the plaintiff. The deponent should explain any delay in bringing the proceedings and the reason for giving any assistance to the occupiers.

That he does not know the name of any person occupying the land who is not named in the summons

As has already been noted,[7] there is no longer any requirement on a plaintiff to take reasonable steps to identify any defendants. Thus, early judicial strictures as to the adequacy of any attempts by the plaintiff to identify occupants have now been superseded.[8]

Notwithstanding this, in view of the strict construction placed by the court on the provisions of the summary pro-

---

6. See above, Chapter 3, page 22.
7. See above, Chapter 5, page 36.
8. See eg *Re 9 Orpen Road, Stoke Newington* [1971] 1 All ER 944, [1971] 1 WLR 166.

cedure, a plaintiff's application may fail should he omit to name in the proceedings any occupier whose identity is in fact known to him, or any servant or agent of his, a problem particularly likely to affect a corporate plaintiff. A deponent should, therefore, state that he does not know the name of any person not named in the application, despite having enquired (if that be the case). If a plaintiff has sought names and these have been refused, he should depose to this.

The subject of unlawful re-occupation of premises at a later date is considered later in this book.[9] Since in the event of any such re-occupation the court has to be satisfied (at any rate in relation to unnamed occupiers) that there exists some nexus between the circumstances of the original entry and the subsequent occupation, every opportunity should be taken to set out as much material relating to identification as possible.

Occupied solely

It will be recalled that the plaintiff must show that the land is 'occupied solely by a person or persons . . . who entered into or remained in occupation without his licence or consent . . .'[10] It is therefore essential for a deponent to state that the land in question is only so occupied.

---

9. See below, Chapter 13.
10. RSC Order 113, rule 1: CCR 1981, Order 24, rule 1.

Chapter 7

Applications for abridgment of time

In the High Court

Order 113, rule 6(1) as amended reads:

> 'A final order for possession in proceedings under this Order shall, except in case of emergency and by leave of the court, not be made—
> (a) in the case of residential premises, less than five clear days after the date of service, and
> (b) in the case of other land, less than two clear days after the date of service.'

Computation of time

The expression 'clear days' means that the period between service of the proceedings and the hearing date is counted by excluding from the computation both the day of service and the day of the hearing. It should be particularly noted that Saturday, Sunday, any bank holiday, Christmas Day and Good Friday are excluded when computing the period, whether it be five or two days.[1]

---

1. RSC Order 3, rule 2.

The inclusion in rule 6(1) of the phrase 'except in case of emergency and by leave of the Court' has the result that if an application for possession is so urgent that the plaintiff fears prejudice by having to wait for the prescribed period of clear days to elapse, he may apply to the court for leave to abridge the period between service and the hearing.

The application is made ex parte to the judge, master or district registrar at or any time after the issue of the originating summons and almost invariably before the hearing of the summons itself.

Mode of application

No procedure is laid down in the rule, but the established practice is for a short affidavit to be sworn, perhaps by the plaintiff's solicitor, setting out the case for abridgment. Unless the plaintiff's affidavit fully discloses the evidence of urgency, the Court will not make the order for abridgment.[2] Grounds for abridgment may include the likelihood of injury to persons (including the defendants) or to property, risk of

---

2. *Westminster City Council v Monahan* [1981] 1 All ER 1050, [1981] 1 WLR 698, CA. The criticism made by the CA in this case of the practice of applying for abridgment before the hearing of the summons rather than at the hearing itself has not led to any change in the practice, which is as noted above. The criticism was partly based on the then current practice in the Ch D supported by *Practice Direction* (Possession of land: RSC Order 113) [1970] 3 All ER 240, [1970] 1 WLR 1250. This, however, was revoked by *Practice Direction* (Chancery Procedure) [1983] 1 All ER 131; [1983] 1 WLR 4, since when relatively few applications under Order 113 have been heard by Ch D judges, with applications for abridgment being extremely rare. It is expected that Ch D and QBD masters will now follow the practice established by the QBD judges, as did the Ch D judge in *Six Arlington Street Investments Ltd v Persons Unknown* [1987] 1 All ER 474: [1987] 1 WLR 188.

injury to health, serious threats to public order or the risk of a rapid increase in numbers of trespassers. Where squatters are occupying a person's home, this should be plainly stated. A suggested form of affidavit is to be found in Appendix II.[3] If the order is made, it must be drawn up in the usual way and served with the prescribed documents. A suggested form of order is to be found in Appendix II.[4]

In the county court

All the above considerations apply to the county court, except as follows.

Computation of time

By CCR 1981, Order 1, rule 9(4), where any period of time, being three days or less, would include a day on which the court office is closed, that day shall be excluded. Thus, in the case of non-residential land, where the period between service and hearing is two days, the days of closure are *excluded*.[5]

However, those days are *included* in the computation of the five day period for residential premises, so that in the county court, in contrast to the High Court, Saturday, Sunday, any bank holiday, Christmas Day and Good Friday are included.[6]

---

3. See below, page 114.
4. See below, page 116.
5. For the days of closure, see CCR 1981, Order 2, rule 2, reproduced in Appendix I below, pages 91–92.
6. *Croydon London Borough Council v Curtin* (1974) 118 Sol Jo 297, CA.

Mode of application

As in the High Court, no procedure is laid down. Nevertheless, as stated in the notes to CCR 1981, Order 24 rule 5 in the *County Court Practice*, the established practice, in contrast to that in the High Court, is for any application for abridgment of time to be made at the hearing of the originating application.[7]

Failure to justify the case for urgency

If the case for urgency is not made out, the proper course is not to dismiss the application, but to adjourn it so as to allow the appropriate period to expire.[8]

Applications since the 1986 revision

The distinction between 'residential premises' and 'other land' which was introduced by the 1986 revision to the procedure is not expected to lead to difficulties of definition. Where any doubt exists and there is sufficient urgency for the distinction to be important, it is suggested that an application to abridge time should be made, at which the court may be asked to rule on the category of premises, albeit that in the High Court any such ruling will be made ex parte.

---

7. The practice in the county court thus follows that approved by CA in *Westminster City Council v Monahan*, ibid, and it remains to be seen whether this unfortunate divergence between the two courts will continue. Providing a judge or registrar can be available outside usual sitting days, there would seem to be no reason why the QB practice should not be followed.
8. See *Westminster City Council v Monahan*, ibid.

The shortening of the return period in non-residential cases to two days is likely to remove the need to apply to abridge time in the majority of cases. Nevertheless, where, for example, a weekend or bank holiday period intervenes, so that the two day period effectively becomes one of four days or more, such an application may still be necessary.

Chapter 8

Service of proceedings

In the High Court

Order 113, rule 4(1) and (2) provides—

(1) Where any person in occupation of the land is named in the originating summons, the summons together with a copy of the affidavit in support shall be served on him:—

    (a) personally, or

    (b) by leaving a copy of the summons and of the affidavit or sending them to him, at the premises, or

    (c) in such other manner as the Court may direct;

(2) Where any person not named as a defendant is in occupation of the land, the summons shall be served (whether or not it is also required to be served in accordance with paragraph (1)), unless the court otherwise directs, by—

    (a) affixing a copy of the summons and a copy of the affidavit to the main door or other conspicuous part of the premises and, if practicable, inserting through the letter-box at the premises a copy of the summons and a copy of

> the affidavit enclosed in a sealed transparent envelope addressed to 'the occupiers', or
> (b) placing stakes in the ground at conspicuous parts of the occupied land, to each of which shall be affixed a sealed transparent envelope addressed to 'the occupiers' and containing a copy of the summons and a copy of the affidavit.

There are two codes, depending on whether the defendants are named or not.

Named defendants

Order 113, rule 4(1) deals with named defendants. Service is to be effected on such defendants personally, by leaving at or sending to the premises a copy of the originating summons (*which must be sealed*)[1] and of the affidavit in support, or in such other manner as the court may direct. If an order for abridgment of time has been obtained, this should be served at the same time.

Unnamed defendants

Order 113, rule 4(2) deals with service on any person not named as a defendant. The plaintiff is required either to affix a sealed copy of the summons and a copy of the affidavit in support to the main door or other conspicuous part of the premises and, if practicable, to insert through any letter-box at the premises a copy of the same documents enclosed in a sealed transparent envelope addressed to 'the occupiers', or to place stakes in the ground at conspicuous parts of the

---

1. RSC Order 113, rule 4(2A).

occupied land and to affix to each of them in a sealed transparent envelope a copy of the same documents, addressed to 'the occupiers'. The mode of service prescribed by the latter alternative was added by the 1986 revision and corresponds closely to the form of order for service on non-residential land commonly made on applications for directions for service prior to the revision.

In the county court

As a result of the 1987 County Court Rules revision, the provisions for service are identical to those in the High Court except that—
1. Notice of the return date must also be delivered to named defendants and
2. Documents to be left at or sent to the premises must be so left or so sent *by an officer of the court*.

The new paragraph (2): a welcome simplification

There are a number of points to be noticed about the new paragraph (2).
1. The new wording achieves a greater clarity of distinction between named and unnamed occupiers for the purposes of service, thereby bringing about a welcome simplification of a rule which has caused practitioners difficulty in the past.

2. The requirements of paragraph (2) are no longer imposed as an *additional* requirement to those of paragraph (1), so that where all the occupiers of the land are named in the summons paragraph (2) will have no application, whatever the nature of the premises.

3. Where any of the occupiers is unnamed, however, two alternative modes of service are prescribed – the paragraph (2)(a) method (previously prescribed) of affixing the documents to the premises or inserting them through the letter-box; and the paragraph (2)(b) method (which is new) of placing stakes in the ground at conspicuous parts of the land to which shall be affixed a sealed transparent envelope addressed to 'the occupiers' and containing the documents referred to above.

These are true alternatives and it will be for the plaintiff to choose which method he adopts. There is no presumption of preference arising from the order in which the alternatives are set out in the rule: *Crosfield Electronics Ltd v Baginsky*.[2] The new alternative of (2)(b) will be particularly welcome to owners of non-residential land who have in the past had to incur the expense and delay of applying to the court for directions for service even in very straightforward cases.

4. Where there are both named and unnamed occupiers, the named occupiers must be served in accordance with paragraph (1) and the proceedings must also be served in accordance with paragraph (2) using, as mentioned in (3) above, whichever alternative is thought to be appropriate.

5. The new paragraph (2) requires the envelope to be not only sealed but *transparent* in both modes of service where unnamed occupiers are in occupation (the former rule simply prescribed that the envelope should be sealed). In view of the strict construction placed by the courts on the

---

2. [1975] 3 All ER 97, [1975] 1 WLR 1135.

provisions of the summary procedure[3] service will be bad if an envelope is used which is not transparent.

6. The new paragraph (2) makes no mention of the number of stakes that should be placed in the ground, save that there must obviously be at least two. The practitioner anxious to avoid argument, therefore, must be careful to ensure that a sufficient number of stakes is used. This will depend on the area of land, the number of occupiers and where they are located. The particular physical and geographical circumstances of any trespass to open land vary too widely for any specific guidance as to the number of stakes to be usefully offered here. Since the rule *requires* only two posts, that may be deemed sufficient under all circumstances. It is suggested, however, that a common sense approach should be adopted and that enough posts be used to ensure that the defendants, wherever they are located, are likely to receive notice of the proceedings. This may in some cases call for substantially more than two stakes. Wherever there is an obvious entrance to the land, one of the stakes should be placed at or near that entrance.

Application for directions for service

As already noted, much costly time and effort were formerly expended in obtaining special directions for the mode of service now provided for in rule 4(2)(b). Clearly, that sort of application will no longer normally be necessary. However, where persons are named, and service on them as provided for in rule 4(2)(a) is not practicable, for example because of

---

3. See *Wiltshire County Council v Frazer* (1983) 82 LGR 313, 47 P & CR 69, CA.

problems of identification, large numbers of defendants, danger to process servers and the like, an application for directions may still be necessary.

Practice

The application both in the High Court and the county court is made ex parte, supported by affidavit stating why compliance with the rules is impracticable, specifying the terms of the order sought and how in the deponent's belief the defendants will receive notice of the proceedings. If the order is made, it should be drawn up and served with the prescribed documents in the manner directed by the order. A suggested form of affidavit and draft order will be found in Appendix II.[4]

Arranging service

As in any other civil proceedings, the plaintiff may serve the originating process himself. Where possession of residential property is claimed, this is entirely appropriate. In cases of mass trespass, or where any difficulty is anticipated, however, it is the writers' experience that the expense of a professional process server is usually justified. It is essential that this part of the procedure is complied with in every respect, since any error or omission may invalidate the proceedings, or at best result in an adjournment for further attempts at service to be made.

---

4. See below, pages 114–116.

A suggested letter of instructions to the plaintiff or process server will be found in Appendix II.[5]

Affidavit of service

Surprisingly, the rules are silent as to the need to prove due service. However, given that in most cases defendants do not appear, the established practice is for an affidavit of service to be sworn and filed, or handed in at the final hearing, a practice which should be followed in every case. A suggested form of affidavit will be found in Appendix II.[6]

---

5. See below, pages 117–119.
6. See below, pages 120–121.

Chapter 9

The hearing

Preparations: a checklist

Although the procedural requirements of Order 113 and
CCR 1981, Order 24 are strict, there are no preparations for
the hearing which are unique to the Order. The following is
a checklist of matters that should be attended to or considered before the hearing.

Plaintiff

1. In the High Court, the summons will ordinarily be listed
   for hearing before a master or district registrar. If the
   nature of the case is such as to raise issues of importance
   or difficulty, arrangements should be made with the listing officer to bring it before a judge.
2. File, or have available to hand in, the affidavit of service.
   Check that the appropriate period between service and
   hearing has elapsed.
3. Have available any deeds or other evidence of title
   referred to in the plaintiff's affidavit.
4. Alert the sheriff or bailiff.[1]

---

1. See below, Chapter 12.

Defendant

1. A person occupying the land who is not named as a
   defendant may, if he wishes to be heard on the question
   whether an order for possession should be made, apply at
   any stage to be joined as a defendant.[2] A consequence of
   being joined is that any named defendant may be ordered
   to pay costs. In practice, the court will enquire whether
   any unnamed occupiers are present, and if so, whether
   they wish to be heard and will not ordinarily hear repre-
   sentations from unnamed persons, unless they apply to
   be joined. The court should warn such unnamed
   occupiers of their potential liability for costs, should they
   be joined.
2. Any named defendant (or unnamed occupier applying to
   be joined) who wishes to assert a defence to the claim for
   possession should, if time permits, set out that defence in
   an affidavit and serve it on the plaintiff. A suggested form
   of affidavit will be found in Appendix II.[3]

Hearing in open court

In the Queen's Bench Division the hearing is in chambers,
unless the court considers that it should be adjourned into
court by reason of its importance or for any other reason.[4] In
the Chancery Division, also, the hearing is in chambers, but
may be adjourned into court.[5] One advantage of a hearing in
open court is the opportunity given for accurate reporting of
the proceedings and any party may make application for
such a hearing. Private hearings in chambers in the Queen's

---

2. RSC Order 113, rule 5; CCR 1981, Order 24, rule 4.
3. See below, pages 110–113.
4. RSC Order 32, rule 13.
5. RSC Order 32, rule 18.

Bench Division are a legacy from the days when juries heard civil cases and are an anachronism so far as Order 113 applications are concerned. They also tend to be unpopular amongst defendants and many sections of the public who regard them as smacking of 'secret justice.'[6] For that reason, it is submitted, the court should readily accede to an unopposed application for the hearing to be in open court. In the county court, the hearing is always in open court.

Application for adjournment

A common application made by defendants at the hearing is for an adjournment. Where such an application is made, the court should enquire carefully into the grounds of the application and, unless the defendant can show the likelihood of a colourable defence or triable issue,[7] his application will normally be refused. The court may hear oral evidence on an application for an adjournment or on the application for possession itself. The court rarely admits evidence from a plaintiff on the application for possession, but may hear oral evidence from a defendant who asserts that there is an issue which ought not to be tried summarily. By testing a defendant's case in this way, the court will be in a position properly to exercise its discretion whether to continue with the summary hearing.

---

6. The Bar Council has urged that they be ended: see *The Times* 4 March, 1987.

7. Even where a triable issue can be shown, it does not follow either that an adjournment will be granted, or that the Court will decline to hear the matter under the summary procedure: see above Chapter 4; but a master or district registrar may refer it to a judge if he thinks it should properly be decided by the judge: RSC Order 113, rule 1A. Homelessness pleaded as necessity is no defence: *Southwark London Borough Council v Williams* [1971] Ch 734, [1971] 2 All ER 175, CA.

The Order for possession

Date

For the manner in which the court can exercise its power to specify a date for possession to be given, see above, Chapter 2, pages 11 and 14. Notwithstanding that the court's hands are tied as regards those who entered as trespassers, in practice there can be flexibility if the plaintiff (a) consents to a short suspension of the order, or (b) uses his discretion as to the date of its execution.

Form of the Order

In the High Court, this is in Form No. 42A of Appendix A to the RSC[8] and in the county court Form N36 of the County Court Forms.[9]

Sunday service

If the case is so urgent that it may be necessary to execute the writ or warrant of possession on a Sunday, an application for Sunday service should be made and, if leave is granted, the order for possession drawn up accordingly.[10]

Costs

There are no special provisions about these in the summary

---

8. For the form, see below, page 95.
9. For the form, see below, page 99.
10. See RSC Order 65, rule 10; CCR 1981, Order 7, rule 3.

procedure and reference should be made to RSC Order 62 and CCR 1981, Order 38. As already stated, costs may be ordered against named defendants, in which event the court will invariably assess them, rather than order a taxation.

Chapter 10

Setting aside the Order and appeal

SETTING ASIDE

By Order 113, rule 8 and CCR 1981, Order 24, rule 7 the court may on such terms as it thinks just, set aside or vary any order made in summary possession proceedings. The appropriate course for anyone aggrieved by the terms of a final order for possession is in the first place to consider applying to the court that made the order.

If he was not a party to the proceedings, then he must apply to be joined.[1]

Practice

The practice is for application to be by summons or notice served on the opposite party and supported by an affidavit.[2]

---

1. RSC Order 113, rule 5; CCR 1981, Order 24, rule 4.
2. For a form of affidavit, see below, pages 110–111.

Principles on which the court acts

This part of the summary jurisdiction has some similarities to the procedure for setting aside judgment.[3] The power to set aside will only be exercised for good cause. The person aggrieved should, therefore, deal in his affidavit with the following points:

1. (If this be the case) the reason for his having taken no part in the proceedings leading to the making of the order;
2. That he has a defence which he would have advanced had he been present;
3. That there are changed circumstances, making it just that the order should be set aside.

APPEAL

High Court

From the master or district registrar

Appeal lies without leave to the judge. The notice must be issued within five days after judgment (seven days from the district registrar) and the appeal is by way of rehearing. Unless the court otherwise directs, an appeal will not operate as a stay.[4]

From the judge

An order for possession made by the Queen's Bench judge in chambers is a final one. Appeal therefore lies to the Court of

---

3. See RSC Order 13, rule 9; cf CCR 1981, Order 37.
4. RSC Order 58, rules 1 and 3.

Appeal without leave.[5] Nor is leave necessary for an appeal from an order made by a judge in the Chancery Division.[6]

The time for service of a notice of appeal is within four weeks from the date on which the order was sealed.[7] Unless otherwise directed, an appeal will not operate as a stay.[8]

County court

From the registrar

Appeal lies to the judge. Notice of appeal must be issued and served within fourteen days of the order.[9]

From the judge

Appeal lies to the Court of Appeal, without leave.[10] The time for service of a notice of appeal is within four weeks from the date of pronouncement of the order and unless otherwise directed, such service does not operate as a stay.[11]

Principles on which the Court of Appeal acts

The usual principles apply. A judge's finding of fact or

---

5. RSC Order 58, rule 6(1) and Supreme Court Act 1981, s 18.
6. Supreme Court Act 1981, s 18.
7. RSC Order 59, rule 4(1).
8. RSC Order 59, rule 13.
9. CCR 1981 Order 37, rule 6(1) and (2).
10. County Courts Act 1984, s 77.
11. RSC Order 59, rule 19 (3) and (5).

exercise of discretion as to fact will only rarely be interfered with; an exercise of discretion as to law is more readily reviewable.[12]

---

12. And see above, Chapter 4.

Part three
Enforcement of the order
for possession

Chapter 11

Essential documents

High Court

After the order for possession has been drawn up, the writ of possession may be issued. This is in Form No 66A of Appendix A to the RSC.[1] It may be issued without leave up to three months from the date of the order for possession.[2] After that time, leave is necessary. The application for leave is made ex parte unless the court otherwise directs.[3] It is suggested that where large areas of land are covered by the writ, the description of the land by reference to its description in the affidavit supporting the originating summons may be appropriate. When issuing the writ of possession, a praecipe for writ of possession (Form PF 81) is also necessary – fee currently £6.00.

---

1. See below, page 96.
2. RSC Order 113, rule 7(1).
3. Ibid.

County court

The order for possession is in Form N36 of the County Court Forms[4] and is drawn up by the court. Execution of the order is by the county court bailiff, following the issue of the warrant of possession in Form N52.[5] This is prepared by the court on receipt of a Request for Warrant in Form N325. The fee currently payable on the Request for the warrant is £25.00.

---

4. See below, page 99.
5. See below, page 100.

Chapter 12

The sheriff and the bailiff

It is important to understand that in the execution of the writ or the warrant the sheriff or bailiff is acting as the court's officer and, as such, is answerable to the court. This may appear so obvious as not to require stating, but in summary possession cases a problem often arises in that the plaintiff, having successfully invoked a rapid procedure to gain an order for possession, then complains of delay in the process of execution. When once the writ or warrant is delivered to the sheriff or bailiff, he is entirely responsible (subject to the court) for the mode and speed of its execution. A detailed discussion of the powers and duties of sheriffs and bailiffs is beyond the scope of this book and reference should be made to 42 *Halsbury's Laws* (4th edn) and *Mather on Sheriff and Execution Law*, (3rd edn, 1935). The following points are, however, offered as guidelines.

THE SHERIFF

Informing the sheriff

If a particular execution is liable to cause difficulty because of the numbers of defendants, the nature of the land or premises, or for any other reason, the plaintiff should inform the sheriff, his deputy or officer as near to the commencement of the proceedings as possible that his services may be required. Although the authority of the sheriff derives solely from the writ of possession, he may need to make plans in advance and the sooner these can be commenced the sooner the writ can be executed.

Delivery of the writ

In the majority of cases, delivery of the writ, together with a clear plan[1] of the land and, in an exceptionally urgent case, the affidavit evidence of urgency,[2] is effected by post or physical delivery. Where a case has been heard in London concerning land at a distance and where urgent execution is desired, the provisions of the Sheriffs Act 1887, s 24 should be noted. Under this section, the sheriff is required to appoint a deputy residing or having an office within a mile from Inner Temple Hall. The delivery of a writ to the London deputy operates as a delivery to the sheriff[3] and the writ obtains priority as from the time of delivery.

Protection of the criminal law: the role of the police

Any person who resists or intentionally obstructs any person who is in fact an officer of a court engaged in executing any process issued by the High Court or any county court for the

---

1. The usual practice is for a plan to accompany the writ: *Six Arlington Street Investments Ltd v Persons Unknown* [1987] 1 All ER 474 at 475; [1987] 1 WLR 188 at 190.
2. Ibid.
3. *Woodland v Fuller* (1840) 11 Ad & El 859 at 867.

purpose of enforcing any judgment or order for the recovery
or delivery of possession of premises is guilty of an offence
and may be arrested without warrant by any police officer in
uniform or officer of the court who reasonably suspects him
to be guilty of the offence.[4] 'Officer of the Court' means any
sheriff, under sheriff, deputy sheriff, bailiff or sheriff's officer
and any bailiff or other person who is an officer of a county
court.[5] It is a defence for an accused to prove that he
believed that the person he was resisting or obstructing was
not an officer of a court.[6] Also, at common law and by virtue
of the Sheriffs Act 1887, s 8(2) the sheriff may call upon the
police for assistance. Although it is the responsibility of the
sheriff to call for that assistance and the police have no duty
as such to the plaintiff, if no previous contact has been made
with them it may be wise at this stage to inform them of the
forthcoming execution of the writ of possession. This will
tend to minimise delay once the writ has been delivered by
giving those concerned ample opportunity to prepare any
plans that may be necessary for the speedy and peaceful
execution of the court's order. However, there will be many
cases where the attendance of the police is wholly
unnecessary.

The extent of the sheriff's duties

The writ of possession is a direction to the sheriff to enter the
land in question and cause the plaintiff to have possession of
it.

---

4. Criminal Law Act 1977, s 10(1) and (5), an offence limited to
resisting or obstructing enforcement of orders obtained under the
summary procedure, for which it was specially created.
5. Ibid, s 10(6).
6. Ibid, s 10(3).

The sheriff is entitled to evict anyone he finds on the premises, even though that person was not a party to the proceedings for possession.[7]

Cases involving trespass by defendants with vehicles, caravans or other heavy chattels or equipment can cause difficulty when execution of the writ is required. Whilst the sheriff may turn out, by force if need be, any person found on land covered by the writ,[8] it appears that he is not under any duty to remove vehicles. The execution of his writ is not complete, however, until quiet possession has been delivered to the plaintiff. It is therefore prudent in cases where difficulty in removal is anticipated:

(a) to define clearly, well in advance, precisely what the sheriff intends to do and what, if any, facilities he will provide;

(b) to advise the plaintiff to provide the means whereby any vehicles, chattels or equipment on land which are immobile can be removed and if necessary stored, away from the land, until either claimed or disposed of. Whilst in practice some sheriffs provide equipment for the removal of such items, it is usually quicker and cheaper for the plaintiff to make such equipment available himself.

Where the sheriff is dilatory

The sheriff's duty to execute a writ of possession, in common

---

7. *R v Wandsworth County Court, ex p London Borough of Wandsworth* [1975] 3 All ER 390, [1975] 1 WLR 1314.

8. *Upton and Wells* Case 1589 1 Leon 145; *R v Wandsworth County Court, ex p London Borough of Wandsworth* [1975] 3 All ER 390, [1975] 1 WLR 1314.

with other writs of execution, is to execute the writ as soon as reasonably practicable and not immediately, without interval of time, whatever the circumstances may be.[9] If he delays, the plaintiff may seek a mandatory injunction against him or bring an action for damages.[10] Presumably, judicial review is also available against the sheriff, but there appears to be no reported instance of its use.

Sheriff's fees

The sheriff or his officer is entitled to receive only such fees and poundage for execution of a writ as may be prescribed.[11]

Currently, these are as follows:
(a) mileage, 22.3p per mile;
(b) incidental expenses and charges. In the absence of an agreement and, in a case where there is no prescribed fee, this shall be such sum as may be allowed on a special application to a Supreme Court master or a district registrar;[12]
(c) poundage: where property is rated, the rate of poundage is 3 per cent of the net annual value for rating of the property seized.[13]

Where unrated land is concerned, the principle of charging generally appears to vary in different parts of England and Wales and an enquiry to the sheriff is recommended.

---

9. *Six Arlington Street Investments Ltd v Persons Unknown* [1987] 1 All ER 474, 475; 1 WLR 188.
10. *Mason v Paynter* (1841) 1 QB 974, 10 LJQB 299; *Six Arlington Street Investments Ltd v Persons Unknown* ibid.
11. Sheriffs Act 1887, s 20(2).
12. Order dated 2nd May 1921, SR & O 192 No 827.
13. Order dated July 8, 1920 as amended by SI 1973/981.

THE COUNTY COURT BAILIFF

Much of the above concerning the powers and duties of the sheriff applies to the county court bailiff.[14] The bailiff, however, has no statutory or common law right to call on the police for assistance, but does have the protection afforded by the Criminal Law Act 1977, s 10. The result is that the bailiff and his officers must ordinarily carry out an eviction themselves, but in the knowledge that police help can be summoned should they meet intentional resistance or obstruction.

---

14. For the responsibility of the bailiff, see County Courts Act 1984, Part VIII.

Chapter 13

Re-occupation by unlawful occupiers: restitution

In the High Court

When a writ of possession has been executed and the sheriff's return made, his function is at an end. However, it may happen that premises or land covered by the original order for possession are re-occupied by trespassers. Providing certain matters can be proved by the dispossessed plaintiff to the court's satisfaction, leave to issue a writ of restitution, which is a supplementary writ in aid of the execution of the writ of possession, may be granted. The writ requires the sheriff to re-enter the premises or land and re-take them for the plaintiff. This remedy, which has perhaps been somewhat neglected by practitioners until recently, is extremely swift and effective, affording the plaintiff repossession within hours of the re-occupation, providing the necessary leave can be obtained.

In cases where the defendants to the original action were named and the plaintiff can assert that those now re-occupying the land are all or some of the same, leave to issue the writ of restitution should be readily granted. A problem may arise, however, in cases of mass trespass where the original occupiers were all, or nearly all, 'persons unknown', and those re-occupying cannot be identified as having been in occupation at the time of the original proceedings. This problem was recently addressed by Simon Brown J in *Wiltshire County Council v Frazer (No 2)*[1] who held that providing there exists a plain and sufficient nexus between the order for possession and the circumstances of the re-occupation, leave to issue a writ of restitution may be granted. The circumstances in which the court's discretion to grant leave are to be exercised were considered by the judge at [1986] 1 All ER 68; [1986] 1 WLR 113, when he said:

> 'In my judgment this will always depend on the particular facts of the individual case, but in exercising its discretion, the court will clearly be concerned above all to consider the extent of any links between the circumstances of adverse possession now obtaining and those which gave rise to the original court order and its earlier execution. The writ of restitution being 'in aid of execution', it would be appropriate to permit its issue only in those cases where there was a plain and sufficient nexus between the original recovery of possession and the need to effect further recovery of the same land.'

Examples of this nexus are evidence of the movement of groups of people of similar lifestyle around the area of the re-occupied land, admissions by persons now in occupation of the land that they knew of the existence of the original order and evidence of identification by the plaintiff of persons or vehicles.

---

1. [1986] 1 All ER 65; [1986] 1 WLR 109.

Practice

The application for leave to issue the writ is ex parte on affidavit to the master or district registrar, unless the court directs it to be on summons.[2] It is not necessary to draw up the order giving leave. The affidavit, endorsed with the order, should be produced, together with the original order, the writ of restitution which must be in Form No 68 to Appendix A to RSC[3] and a praecipe for the writ of restitution (No PF 91 suitably adapted) and stamped £6.

The sheriff's duties in executing the writ of restitution are identical to those in executing the writ of possession.

In the county court

The county court has power to give leave to issue a warrant of restitution in identical circumstances.[4]

Practice

The application for leave is made ex parte, with a supporting affidavit giving evidence of wrongful re-entry on to the land since the execution of the warrant of possession.[5] The warrant is in Form N51 of the County Court Forms, issued by the court.[6]

It will be clear from the above that if the plaintiff is doubtful of his chance of satisfying the court of the existence of the necessary nexus, he will have no option but to start fresh proceedings.

---

2. RSC Order 46, rule 4.
3. This form is reproduced below, page 97.
4. CCR 1981, Order 26, rule 17(4).
5. Ibid, rule 17(5).
6. This form is reproduced below, page 102.

Appendices

Appendix I

Rules of Court

1. RSC Order 113
2. CCR 1981, Order 24.
3. CCR 1981, Order 2, rule 2.

RSC ORDER 113

Proceedings to be brought by originating summons

1. Where a person claims possession of land which he alleges is occupied solely by a person or persons (not being a tenant or tenants holding over after the termination of the tenancy) who entered into or remained in occupation without his licence or consent or that of any predecessor in title of his, the proceedings may be brought by originating summons in accordance with the provisions of this Order.

Jurisdiction of masters

1A. Proceedings under this Order may be heard and determined by a master, who may refer them to a judge if he thinks they should properly be decided by the judge.

Form of originating summons

2. The originating summons shall be in Form No. 11A in Appendix A and no acknowledgment of service shall be required.

Affidavit in support

3. The plaintiff shall file in support of the originating summons an affidavit stating—
  (*a*) his interest in the land;
  (*b*) the circumstances in which the land has been occupied without licence or consent and in which his claim to possession arises; and
  (*c*) that he does not know the name of any person occupying the land who is not named in the summons.

Service of originating summons

4.—(1) Where any person in occupation of the land is named in the originating summons, the summons together with a copy of the affidavit in support shall be served on him—
  (*a*) personally; or
  (*b*) by leaving a copy of the summons and of the affidavit or sending them to him, at the premises; or
  (*c*) in such other manner as the Court may direct.
(2) Where any person not named as a defendant is in occupation of the land, the summons shall be served (whether or not it is also required to be served in accordance with paragraph (1)), unless the court otherwise directs, by—
  (*a*) affixing a copy of the summons and a copy of the affidavit to the main door or other conspicuous part of the premises and, if practicable, inserting through the letter-box at the premises a copy of the summons and a copy of the affidavit enclosed in a sealed transparent envelope addressed to 'the occupiers'; or
  (*b*) placing stakes in the ground at conspicuous parts of the occupied land, to each of which shall be affixed

a sealed transparent envelope addressed to 'the occupiers' and containing a copy of the summons and a copy of the affidavit.

(2A) Every copy of an originating summons for service under paragraph (1) or (2) shall be sealed with the seal of the Office of the Supreme Court out of which the summons was issued.

(3) Order 28, rule 3 shall not apply to proceedings under this Order.

Application by occupier to be made a party

5. Without prejudice to Order 15, rules 6 and 10, any person not named as a defendant who is in occupation of the land and wishes to be heard on the question whether an order for possession should be made may apply at any stage of the proceedings to be joined as a defendant.

Order for possession

6.—(1) A final order for possession in proceedings under this Order shall, except in case of emergency and by leave of the court, not be made–
  (*a*) in the case of residential premises, less than five clear days after the date of service, and
  (*b*) in the case of other land, less than two clear days after the date of service.

(2) An order for possession in proceedings under this Order shall be in Form No. 42A.

(3) Nothing in this Order shall prevent the Court from ordering possession to be given on a specified date, in the exercise of any power which could have been exercised if possession had been claimed in an action begun by writ.

Writ of possession

7.—(1) Order 45, rule 3(2) shall not apply in relation to an order for possession under this Order but no writ of possession to enforce such an order shall be issued after the expiry of three months from the date of the order without the leave of the Court.

An application for leave may be made *ex parte* unless the Court otherwise directs.

(2) The writ of possession shall be in Form No 66A.

Setting aside order

8. The court may, on such terms as it thinks just, set aside or vary any order made in proceedings under this order.

CCR 1981, ORDER 24

Summary proceedings for the recovery of land

Proceedings to be by originating application

1. Where a person claims possession of land which he alleges is occupied solely by a person or persons (not being a tenant or tenants holding over after the termination of the tenancy) who entered into or remained in occupation without his licence or consent or that of any predecessor in title of his, the proceedings may be brought by originating application in accordance with the provisions of this Order.

Affidavit in support

2. The applicant shall file in support of the originating application an affidavit stating—

(*a*) his interest in the land;

(*b*) the circumstances in which the land has been occupied without licence or consent and in which his claim to possession arises; and

(*c*) that he does not know the name of any person occupying the land who is not named in the originating application.

Service of originating application

3.—(1) Where any person in occupation of the land is named in the originating application, the application shall be served on him—

(*a*) by delivering to him personally a copy of the originating application, together with the notice of the return day required by Order 3, rule 4(4)(b), and a copy of the affidavit in support; or

(*b*) by an officer of the court leaving the documents mentioned in subparagraph (a), or sending them to him, at the premises; or

(*c*) in accordance with Order 7, rule 11, as applied to originating applications by Order 3, rule 4(6); or

(*d*) in such other manner as the court may direct.

(2) Where any person not named as a respondent is in occupation of the land, the originating application shall be served (whether or not it is also required to be served in accordance with paragraph (1)), unless the court otherwise directs, by

(*a*) affixing a copy of each of the documents mentioned in paragraph (1)(*a*) to the main door or other conspicuous part of the premises and, if practicable, inserting through the letter-box at the premises a copy of those documents enclosed in a sealed transparent envelope addressed to 'the occupiers'; or (*b*) placing stakes in the ground at conspicuous parts of the occupied land, to each of which shall be affixed a sealed transparent envelope addressed to 'the occupiers' and containing a copy of each of the documents mentioned in paragraph (1)(a);[1]

Application by occupier to be made a party

4. Without prejudice to Order 15, rule 1, any person not named as a respondent who is in occupation of the land and wishes to be heard on the question whether an order for possession should be made may apply at any stage of the proceedings to be joined as respondent, and the notice of the return day required by Order 3, rule 4 (4)(b) shall contain a notice to that effect.

Hearing of originating application

5.—(1) Except in case of urgency and by leave of the court, the day fixed for the hearing of the originating application

(*a*) in the case of residential premises, shall not be less than 5 days after the day of service, and

(*b*) in the case of other land, shall not be less than 2 days after the day of service.[2]

(2) Notwithstanding anything in Order 21, rule 5, no order for possession shall be made on the originating application except by the judge or, with the leave of the judge, by the registrar.

---

1. Paragraph (2) substituted by the County Court (Amendment) Rules 1987, SI 1987/493.

2. Rule 5(1), (*a*) and (*b*) substituted by the County Court (Amendment) Rules 1987, SI 1987/493.

(3) An order for possession in proceedings under this Order shall be to the effect that the plaintiff do recover possession of the land mentioned in the originating application.

(4) Nothing in this Order shall prevent the court from ordering possession to be given on a specified date, in the exercise of any power which could have been exercised if the proceedings had been brought by action.

Warrant of possession

6.—(1) Subject to paragraphs (2) and (3), a warrant of possession to enforce an order for possession under this Order may be issued at any time after the making of the order and subject to the provisions of Order 26, rule 17, a warrant of restitution may be issued in aid of the warrant of possession.

(2) No warrant of possession shall be issued after the expiry of 3 months from the date of the order without the leave of the court, and an application for such leave may be made ex parte unless the court otherwise directs.

(3) Nothing in this rule shall authorise the issue of a warrant of possession before the date on which possession is ordered to be given.

Setting aside order

7. The judge may, on such terms as he thinks just, set aside or vary any order made in proceedings under this Order.

CCR 1981, ORDER 2, RULE 2

Days of opening

2.—(1) Every court office or, if a court has two or more offices, at least one of those offices, shall be open on every day of the year except—

   (*a*)   Saturdays and Sundays,
   (*b*)   the day before Good Friday from noon onwards and Good Friday,
   (*c*)   the Tuesday after the spring holiday,
   (*d*)   Christmas Eve or—
      (i)   if that day is a Saturday, then 23rd December,
      (ii) if that day is a Sunday or a Tuesday, then 27th December,
   (*e*)   Christmas Day and, if that day is a Friday or Saturday, then 28th December,
   (*f*)   bank holidays, and
   (*g*)   such other days as the Lord Chancellor may by general or special order direct.

   (2)   In the foregoing paragraph 'bank holiday' means a bank holiday in England and Wales under the Banking and Financial Dealings Act 1971 and 'spring holiday' means the bank holiday on the last Monday in May or any day appointed instead of that day under section 1(2) of that Act.

Appendix II

Forms and precedents

1. Form No 11A: Originating summons for possession under Order 113
2. Form No 42A: Order for possession under Order 113
3. Form No 66A: Writ of possession under Order 113
4. Form No 68: Writ of restitution
5. Form N312: Originating application for possession under Order 24
6. Form N36: Order for possession under Order 24
7. Form N52: Warrant of possession under Order 24
8. Form N51: Warrant of restitution
9. Draft affidavit in support of originating summons under Order 113—residential property (including assertion of urgency and to abridge time for making order)
10. Draft affidavit in support of originating summons under Order 113 (non-residential land)
11. Draft affidavit in opposition to application for summary order for possession (including an application to be joined as a defendant and to set aside an order already made)
12. Draft affidavit in support of application for abridgment of time for service and directions for service
13. Draft Order for abridgment of time and for special directions as to service
14. Draft letter of instructions to process server
15. Draft affidavit of service
16. Draft affidavit in support of ex parte application for leave to issue writ/warrant of restitution

1. FORM NO 11A

Originating summons for possession under Order 113 (O.113, r2)

Royal Arms

In the High Court of Justice   19   No.
     Division
     In the matter of
[A.B.   Plaintiff
     C.D.   Defendant (if any) whose name is
                             known to the plaintiff]
     To [C.D. and] every [other] person in occupation of
     Let all persons concerned attend before
          Royal Courts of Justice, Strand, London, WC2A 2LL,
on   day, the   day of   19   , at
o'clock, on the hearing of an application by A.B. for an order
that he do recover possession of   on the ground that
he is entitled to possession and that the person(s) in occupation is (are) in occupation without licence or consent.
     Dated the   day of   19   .
     This summons was taken out by   of
solicitor for the said plaintiff whose address is
[*or* This summons was taken out by   of
agent for   of   solicitor for the said plaintiff
whose address is   ] [*or when the plaintiff acts in person*
     This summons was taken out by the said plaintiff who
resides at
and is (*state occupation*) and (*if the plaintiff does not reside within
the jurisdiction*) whose address for service is   ].
     Note—Any person occupying the premises who is not
named as a defendant by this summons may apply to the
Court personally or by counsel or solicitor to be joined as a
defendant. If a person occupying the premises does not
attend personally or by counsel or solicitor at the time and
place above-mentioned, such order will be made as the
Court may think just and expedient.

2. FORM NO 42A

Order for possession under Order 113 (O.113, r6)

[heading as in summons]

Upon hearing   and upon reading the affidavit of
        filed the   day of   19   it is ordered
that the plaintiff A.B. do recover possession of the land
described in the originating summons as   [1] *[and the
defendant*   *do give possession of the said land on*
        ] [and that the defendant   *do pay the plaintiff*
£   *costs [or to be taxed]]*
The above costs, etc. *[as in No 39]*
Dated the   day of   19

---

1. In the case of non-residential land, the following additional informa-
    tion is of assistance in identifying the land covered by the order
        'and shown edged [red] on the plan [ABC 1] annexed to the
    affidavit of [name of plaintiff/deponent] sworn on . . .'

3. FORM NO 66A

Writ of possession under Order 113 (O.113, r7)

[*heading as in summons*]
ELIZABETH THE SECOND [*as in No 53*]
To the Sheriff of   greeting:
Whereas it was on the   day of   19   ordered
that the plaintiff A.B. do recover possession of   [2]
[*describe the land recovery of which has been ordered*] in your county
[and that the defendant C.D. do pay him £   costs [or
costs to be taxed, which costs have been taxed and allowed at
£   as appears by the taxing officer's certificate dated
the   day of 19   ]]
We command you that you enter the said land and cause
A.B. to have possession of it
[And we also command you that of the goods, chattels and
other property [*remainder as in No 53*]]]

---

2. See above note 1 to Form No 42A above, for a suggested addition to
the prescribed form in cases of non-residential land.

4. FORM NO 68

Writ of restitution (O.46, r1)

[*Heading as in action*]
ELIZABETH THE SECOND [*as in No 53*]
To the sheriff of   greeting:

Whereas in the above named action it was on the day of   19   adjudged [*or* ordered] that the defendant C.D. do give the plaintiff A.B. possession of [*describe the land delivery of which was adjudged or ordered*]:

And whereas on the   day of   19   a writ of possession was issued pursuant to the said judgment [*or* order] directing you to give possession of the said land to the said A.B., but it appearing to our High Court of Justice that certain other persons have wrongfully taken possession of the said land and our said Court having on the   day of   19   ordered that a writ of restitution should be issued in respect of the said land:

We command you that you enter the said land and cause A.B. to have restitution thereof.

And we also command you that you indorse [*remainder as in No 53*].

5. FORM N312

Originating application for possession under Order 24 (O. 24, r1)

	In the	**County Court** **Case No.**
IN THE MATTER OF		
BETWEEN	*A.B.* and	*Applicant*
	C.D.	*Respondent if any whose name is known to the Applicant.*

, of   [*state address and occupation of Applicant*] hereby applies to the Court for an order for recovery of possession of

[*here describe the property*] on the ground that he is entitled to possession and that the person[s] in occupation of the premises is [are] in occupation without licence or consent.

The person[s] in occupation who is [are] intended to be served individually with this application is [are]:—

[*here state the name of every person in occupation whose name the applicant knows*]. [*Add where appropriate.* There are other persons in occupation whose names are not known to the applicant]

[*Or* It is not intended to serve any person individually with notice of this application.]

The Applicant's address for service is:—

[*here state the Applicant's address for service*].

DATED

SIGNED   [solicitors for the] APPLICANT

6. FORM N36

Order for possession under Order 24 (O. 24, r5(3))

[*General Title—Form N.200*]

UPON HEARING
[and upon reading the affidavit of
of   ]

IT IS ORDERED that the Applicant   do
recover possession of the land mentioned in the originating
application in this matter, namely [*Here describe the land.*]

[*Where the Respondent is named and the Court exercises its power to
postpone the order add*

AND IT IS ORDERED that the Respondent do give possession
of the land on
                    ]
that the Applicant do recover against the Respondent the
sum of £   for costs [*or* his costs of this matter to be
taxed on scale   ]

AND FURTHER that the Respondent do pay the sum above
mentioned into the office of this Court on or before the
                    [*or* do pay the costs, when taxed into the office
of this Court on or before that day, or, if the costs have not
been taxed before the expiration of that day, within 14 days
of taxation.]

DATED

TAKE NOTICE. This judgment will be registered in the
Register of County Court Judgments if £10 or more remains
outstanding one month after the date of judgment. Registration may affect your ability to obtain credit. You may
apply to the court for the registration to be cancelled when
the judgment has been fully satisfied.

7. FORM N52

Warrant of possession under Order 24 (Ord. 24, r6(1))

In the	**County Court**
	Case No.
	Warrant No.

BETWEEN   *Applicant*

AND   *Respondent*

To the Registrar and Bailiffs of the Court.

ON the   day of   19   , it was ordered that the Applicant do recover possession of [*Describe the land as set out in the order.*]   [and it was ordered that the Applicant do recover against the Respondent the sum of £   for costs, which the Respondent was ordered to pay into the office of this Court on or before the   ].

AND THE RESPONDENT HAVING FAILED TO OBEY THE ORDER THE APPLICANT HAS REQUESTED THAT THIS WARRANT SHOULD ISSUE

YOU ARE THEREFORE REQUIRED TO GIVE POSSESSION OF THE LAND TO THE APPLICANT.

[AND, the Respondent having failed to pay the costs as ordered you are required forthwith to levy the amount due to the Applicant under the order, together with the costs of issue and execution of this warrant by distress and sale of the Respondent's goods, wherever they may be found within the district of this Court (except the wearing apparel and bedding of him or his family to the value of £100, and the tools and implements of his trade to the value of £150), and also by seizing any money, bank notes, bills of exchange, promissory notes, bonds, specialties, or securities for money, belonging to him which may be found there or so much thereof as may be sufficient to satisfy this execution, and to bring the proceeds of the levy into Court, and immediately thereafter to make a return of what you have done.]

Application was made to this court for this Warrant at

minutes past the hour of · · o'clock on
NOTICE. The goods are not to be sold until after the end of
five days next following the day on which they are seized,
unless they are of a perishable nature, or at the request of the
Defendant.

[Notice of Levy—Form N.45]

8. FORM N51

Warrant of restitution (Ord. 24, r6(1))

To the Registrar and Bailiffs of the Court.

ON the   day of   19   , it was ordered that the applicant was entitled to possession of [*Describe the land as set out in the order*].

AND on the   day of   19   , a warrant of possession was issued, pursuant to the   order requiring you to give possession of the   land to the applicant and possession of the land was given by you to the applicant under the warrant on the day of   19   .

AND the applicant having satisfied the Court that the   land has been re-entered wrongfully and the Court having ordered, on the   day of 19   , that a warrant of restitution should issue in respect of the land [and the respondent should pay the applicant the sum of £   for costs].

YOU ARE THEREFORE REQUIRED forthwith to enter the   land and to cause the applicant to have restitution thereof, and forthwith to levy [the sum of £ [*The amount due to the Plaintiff under the order*] together with] the costs of issue and execution of this warrant by distress and sale of the respondant's goods wherever they may be found within the district of this Court (except the wearing apparel and bedding of him or his family to the value of £100 and the tools and implements of his trade to the value of £150), and also be seizing any money, bank notes, bills of exchange, promissory notes, bonds, specialties, or securities for money, belonging to him which may be found there or so much thereof as may be sufficient to satisfy this execution, and to bring the proceeds of the levy into Court, and immediately thereafter to make a return of what you have done.

Application was made to this court for this warrant at minutes past the hour of   o'clock on

NOTICE. The goods are not to be sold until after the end of five days next following the day on which they were seized, unless they are of a perishable nature or at the request of the Applicant.

[Notice of Levy—Form N.45]

9. DRAFT AFFIDAVIT IN SUPPORT OF ORIGINATING SUMMONS UNDER ORDER 113—RESIDENTIAL PROPERTY (INCLUDING ASSERTION OF URGENCY AND TO ABRIDGE TIME FOR MAKING ORDER)

IN THE HIGH COURT OF JUSTICE   1987 M
CHANCERY/QUEEN'S BENCH DIVISION
[MELCHESTER DISTRICT REGISTRY]
IN THE MATTER OF 24 SPIRE VIEW, MELCHESTER, WESSEX
BETWEEN:

> THE MELCHESTER DISTRICT COUNCIL   *Plaintiff*
>   and
> JOHN SMITH
> and
> PERSONS UNKNOWN   *Defendants*
>   AFFIDAVIT OF MICHAEL WILLIAMS

I, MICHAEL WILLIAMS of The Council Offices, Melchester, Wessex, HEREBY MAKE OATH and SAY as follows:

1. I am employed by the Plaintiff as its assistant housing officer. I depose to all the facts in this Affidavit from my own knowledge and perusal of the Plaintiff's records. I am duly authorised to make this Affidavit on the Plaintiff's behalf.

2. 24 Spire View, Melchester ('the property') is a house owned by the Plaintiff. It is normally let on secure tenancies under the provisions of the Housing Act 1985, Section 79. Such a tenancy confers the right upon the tenant for the time being of exclusive possession and the tenant is permitted to take in lodgers without the Plaintiff's prior consent.

3. The property was let on or about the 1st June 1977 to Dora Jane Brown ('Mrs. Brown') in the manner deposed to above. There is now produced and shown to me marked 'MW 1' a true copy of the letting agreement. I am aware

from my perusal of the Plaintiff's records relating to the property that Mrs. Brown had in fact taken in a lodger, who is the named Defendant herein.

4. The Plaintiff was informed on or about   that Mrs. Brown had died. From enquiries I have made, I believe she died intestate.[3] On   I visited the property. I found it still to be occupied by the Defendant, Smith. I informed him that he must vacate the property, but he told me that he was not prepared to go without a Court Order.

5. I instructed the Plaintiff's Solicitors to take all steps to obtain vacant possession of the property and there is now produced and shown to me marked 'MW 2' a true copy of the Notice to Quit served on the President of the Family Division as administrator of the Estate of Mrs. Brown. That Notice expired on   . At the same time, I caused a letter to be written to the Defendant, Smith, informing him of the position and that he must leave the property. A true copy of that letter is now produced and shown to me marked 'MW 3'.

6. On   I again visited the property. I found, in addition to the Defendant, Smith, a number of other persons, apparently living in the property. It was in a filthy condition, with many windows broken and an outer door hanging off its hinges. I attempted to discover the identities of these other persons, but was subjected to abuse and deemed it wise to leave the property. I am unaware of the date or dates these persons arrived, but I can say that no-one has permission to come to live in the property.

---

3. *Wirral Borough Council v Smith* [1982] 80 LGR 628, 43 P & CR 312, CA.

7. Save for the Defendant, Smith, I do not know the name of any other person in the property. I have specifically enquired of colleagues with the Plaintiff Authority and no-one else knows any names either. The property is now occupied solely by persons who remain in it without the licence or consent of the Plaintiff.

8. In view of the damage that is occurring at the property and the obvious diminution in the value of the Plaintiff's property, I respectfully ask the Court to hear this matter as one of urgency,[4] notwithstanding that five days may not have elapsed between the date of service of the proceedings herein and the date of hearing.

[*Sworn*]

---

4. See *Westminster City Council v Monahan* [1981] 1 All ER 1050; [1981] 1 WLR 698, CA. *Note*: This form may be adapted for use in the county court.

10. DRAFT AFFIDAVIT IN SUPPORT OF ORIGINATING SUMMONS UNDER ORDER 113 (NON-RESIDENTIAL LAND)

IN THE HIGH COURT OF JUSTICE 1987
CHANCERY/QUEEN'S BENCH DIVISION
[MELCHESTER DISTRICT REGISTRY]
IN THE MATTER OF GUNTER'S FARM ESTATE, ALDER-BRIDGE, WESSEX
BETWEEN:

JOHN WATNEY	*1st Plaintiff*
EDMUND WHITBREAD	*2nd Plaintiff*
PETER BURTON	*3rd Plaintiff*
and	
PERSONS UNKNOWN	*Defendants*

AFFIDAVIT OF JOHN WATNEY

I, JOHN WATNEY of GUNTER'S FARM, ALDERBRIDGE, Wessex, farmer, HEREBY MAKE OATH and SAY as follows:

1. I am the 1st Plaintiff herein. I depose to the facts hereafter set out from my own knowledge.

2. I am the freehold owner of a mixed farming and sporting estate known as Gunter's Farm Estate, Alderbridge, Wessex. My title is derived from a Conveyance to me dated 14th February 1962. I undertake to produce the original at the hearing of this Summons. There is now produced and shown to me marked 'JW 1' a plan showing edged black the extent of this Estate. I farm the majority of the holding myself and I am therefore entitled to possession of it.

3. The area of land hatched black on 'JW 1' is let on an agricultural lease dated 29th September 1981 to the 2nd Plaintiff. This confers exclusive possession of that area of land on the 2nd Plaintiff. However, Clause 24 of that lease contains a covenant by the 2nd Plaintiff 'to give notice to

trespassers and so far as possible to stop all encroachments and immediately inform the Landlord thereof and to allow the tenant's name to be used in actions (civil or criminal) against any alleged trespasser or poacher on being indemnified against any cost in respect thereof'. I am therefore entitled to proceed with this action in the name of the 2nd Plaintiff.

4. The area of land cross-hatched black is let to the 3rd Plaintiff on an oral grazing licence from March to November each year. The extent to which this confers exclusive possession on the 3rd Plaintiff has never been the subject of discussion between us. For the avoidance of doubt, therefore, the 3rd Plaintiff has been joined as a Plaintiff. I produce marked 'JW 2' an authority signed by the 3rd Plaintiff authorising me to bring this action on his behalf.

5. Gunter's Farm Estate is crossed by a number of public rights of way, both by way of roads and public footpaths. Also, the area of land at the south-west corner of the Estate known as 'Gunters Common' is subject to rights of common in favour of adjoining residents. These are the subject of a registration under the Commons Registration Act 1967. Save to the extent deposed to, there are no other rights conferred on any member of the public to come on to or remain on the said land.

6. On   , I received a report from a member of my staff that a group of people and vehicles had come on to a portion of the said land at a location which was explained to me. I visited this area in the late afternoon of   , and there found a group of about 40 vehicles, consisting of old buses, lorries and cars. In this group there were, I would estimate, about 120 adults and children. Their attitude was not hostile. I therefore asked to speak to their leader and a man with multi-coloured hair came forward. I asked him his name, but he refused to give it. I told him that he and the

others were on private land and that they were trespassing. He said that he was aware that the land was private but that the land on which they were camping was an area traditionally used by travelling people. I informed him that no rights to camp existed over that area or any other within the Estate and that he must leave at once or Court proceedings would follow.

7. On the said plan 'JW 1' the area of land occupied by the Defendants is indicated by the words 'Trespassers here'. The Court will observe that this area encompasses land retained in hand by me, let to the 2nd Plaintiff and occupied by the 3rd Plaintiff.

8. As deposed to in paragraph 6 above, I asked the name of the man to whom I spoke, but this was not given. I know the name of no other member of the group of trespassers. I have enquired specifically of all members of my farm staff and of the 2nd and 3rd Plaintiffs. None of them knows any names either.

9. The land the subject of this application is occupied solely by the Defendants.

10. Although only a portion of the Estate is at present being trespassed upon, because of the number of roads and tracks on it, I fear that the Defendants could with great ease move to another part of the said Estate. I respectfully repeat that none of them has any right to occupy any part of the Estate and if they moved elsewhere, they would be trespassing. For that reason, I would respectfully ask for an Order for possession covering all the land comprising the said Estate.[5]
[*Sworn*]

---

5. See *University of Essex v Djemal* [1980] 2 All ER 742, [1980] 1 WLR 1301, CA: see above, pages 37–38.

11. DRAFT AFFIDAVIT IN OPPOSITION TO APPLICATION FOR SUMMARY ORDER FOR POSSESSION (INCLUDING AN APPLICATION TO BE JOINED AS A DEFENDANT AND TO SET ASIDE AN ORDER ALREADY MADE)

[*Note*: This affidavit contains outlines of some of the defences and triable issues referred to in the text above, and should be expanded and adapted as appropriate]

[*Heading as in the summons/application*]

I, DONALD FARFRAE, at present of [*give address of premises or land of which possession has been claimed*] unemployed, MAKE OATH and SAY as follows:

Application to be made a party

[1. I am not named as a defendant in these proceedings. I am, however, at present living on the land of which the Plaintiff claims possession. I understand that in order to be heard on the question whether an order for possession should be made, I should apply to be joined as a defendant and I hereby so apply[6]]

Application to set aside order

[2. This affidavit is sworn in support of my application to set aside the order of Mr. District Registrar   made on the   . I apologise to the Court that I failed to attend the hearing on that date. I was not in the premises when the proceedings were apparently left at them. I have been informed by the Plaintiff's Solicitors that, as there is no letter-box at the premises, the proceedings were left in an

---

6. See RSC Order 113, rule 5.

envelope attached to the front door. For a reason that I am unable to explain, there were no papers so attached when I returned and thus I was completely unaware of the hearing. Had I been present at the hearing, I would have advanced the matters deposed to below in opposition to the Plaintiff's claim. I now seek to have the matter reheard. I also ask for a stay in the execution of the order for possession]

Licence agreement a sham[7]

[3. I have seen a copy of the Plaintiff's affidavit sworn on the   and of the copy form of licence agreement annexed to this. It is true that I signed the original of that agreement, but I did so under the following circumstances. I was badly in need of accommodation and was introduced to the Plaintiff who said he had a flat vacant. We agreed terms as to rent, use of furniture and other matters. I asked for a rent book. The Plaintiff said that it was not his practice to issue these, as the terms of the mortgage on the property precluded him from granting tenancies. He produced for me to sign the document annexed to his said affidavit. He told me that, whatever its terms, I could regard myself as his tenant. Being so hard-pressed for somewhere to live, I agreed to sign. Since then and contrary to the terms of the agreement, I have paid rent and have exclusive possession of my flat. I allege that the agreement that I signed is a sham and that I am a tenant of the Plaintiff. I am advised that as such, the procedure for summary possession is not available against me and I ask for the Plaintiff's claim to be dismissed.]

---

7. See *Markou v Da Silvaesa, Crancour v Merola* (1986) 52 P & CR 204, CA.

Licence not lawfully terminated[8]

[4. I have seen a copy of the Plaintiff's affidavit filed herein. I accept that I have only a licence to live in the Plaintiff's cottage and that I pay no rent. However, what the Plaintiff has failed to point out is that I have lived in the cottage for over 10 years and, prior to the commencement of these proceedings, I received only two days notice requiring me to leave. I therefore contend that my licence has not been properly terminated and that the Plaintiff is not entitled to possession.]

Land occupied by persons with plaintiff's consent

[5. I have seen a copy of the Plaintiff's Affidavit sworn herein. In paragraph 7 of that he deposes that the land of which he seeks summary possession is occupied solely by the group of people of which I am a part. This is not true. The land has on it two large mobile homes. I have spoken to the occupiers of these and both have shown me letters from the Plaintiff authorising them to be on the land with their caravans. I am advised that because of their presence, the Plaintiff is not entitled to invoke the summary possession procedure against me, or those with me.]

Plaintiff not proper party

[6. In paragraph 4 of his Affidavit sworn in these proceedings, the Plaintiff avers that he is entitled to possession of the premises, the subject of this summons. I believe this not to be true. I now produce maked 'JF 1' a letter from Messrs. Bax

---

8. See *Minister of Health v Bellotti* [1944] KB 298, [1944] 1 All ER 238, CA.

and Stainer, solicitors, confirming that they act for an undisclosed client who has a lease granted by the Plaintiff of the premises in which I am living. Under those circumstances, the Plaintiff is not entitled to possession.]

Trespass ab initio: denial of damage

[7. In paragraph 5 of the Plaintiff's affidavit sworn herein, it is alleged that since I have been on the land of which possession is claimed, I have damaged it by cutting down trees for firewood and by digging holes to bury rubbish. On the basis of that allegation, the Plaintiff asserts that the right given to me as a member of the public to come on to the land by virtue of the access arrangements to which he deposes has come to an end. I strongly deny that I have done any damage, as alleged or at all. I live by myself in a converted ambulance and I always travel alone. I use only fallen wood for cooking and dispose of my litter in bins. When I arrived on the land, I saw clear signs that trees had been damaged and the ground disturbed by digging; this was not done by me and the Plaintiff has produced no evidence that it was. No notice determining the public's right of access to the land has been served on me or brought to my attention and it is my case, therefore, that I am on the land lawfully.]

12. DRAFT AFFIDAVIT IN SUPPORT OF APPLICATION FOR ABRIDGMENT OF TIME FOR SERVICE AND DIRECTIONS FOR SERVICE

[*Heading as summons/application*]
AFFIDAVIT OF ANNA HARNHAM

I, ANNA HARNHAM at present of [give address of premises or land of which possession is claimed] HEREBY MAKE OATH and SAY as follows:

1. I am the Plaintiff and the freehold owner of the property the subject of this application. This affidavit is sworn by me in support of an application for abridgment of time [and for special directions] for service. [Refer to affidavit in support of application.]

Application for abridgment of time

[2. I have again visited the site of the trespass. This visit was this morning, the   . I found the situation at the site much worse than on my previous visit. The number of vehicles has greatly increased. I estimate there are now 60–70 vehicles and about 200 people. On my way to the site, I passed a number of vehicles of a similar type to those already on the site, apparently driving towards it on the public road. The site is immediately next to a field of young corn and also to a field of cattle. I saw extensive evidence of foot and vehicle damage to the corn field and I fear that if the fence around the stock was damaged, the cows will run loose.

3. I fear that irreparable damage may be done to the land and its surroundings if even two days elapse before this application is heard. I am advised by my Solicitors that the earliest this case could normally be heard would be next Tuesday. I therefore respectfully ask for an order abridging time to enable a hearing to take place before the weekend.]
OR

[2. The site immediately adjoins the main railway line from Waterloo to Putney, along stretches of which the wire fence is in very poor repair. The site also has on it a number of half-demolished buildings. The persons trespassing on the site include a number of young children, whom I fear could be injured should they play in the buildings, or stray on to the railway line.]

Application for directions for service

[4. As to service, my Solicitors have informed me of the normal rules prevailing for this. For the following reasons, I believe that such service would not be possible. When I visited the site today, I found the atmosphere to be most hostile. As I drove on to the edge of the site, a large crowd gathered round me. I was subjected to shouts and obscene catcalls. I was told that if I went near the site again, my car would be rolled over and my head punched in. I deemed it advisable at this point to withdraw.

5. I believe that if anyone attempting to serve process went near the site he might be subjected to violence. I believe that if the documents required to be served were attached to posts on either side of the entrance to the site this would bring the proceedings to the attention of the trespassers.]
[*Sworn*]

13. DRAFT ORDER FOR ABRIDGMENT OF TIME AND FOR SPECIAL DIRECTIONS AS TO SERVICE

[Heading as in summons/application]

UPON HEARING Counsel/the Solicitors for the Plaintiffs. AND UPON READING the Affidavit of ANNA HARNHAM sworn on the   and filed herein

IT IS ORDERED:

1. That provided service of the originating summons be effected by not later than 6 pm today that the time for service be abridged so as to enable the hearing of the Plaintiff's summons herein to take place on

2. That service of:
   (a) A sealed copy of the Originating Summons:
   (b) A copy of the Affidavit of ANNA HARNHAM sworn on   (and the exhibits thereto); and
   (c) A copy of this Order

   by the affixing of them to two posts inserted in the ground one at each side of the entrance to the site the subject of these proceedings, shall be good and sufficient service.

DATED the

14. DRAFT LETTER OF INSTRUCTIONS TO PROCESS SERVER

Dear Sir,
         Re: _____
We act for the Plaintiff in these proceedings, which are for summary possession of the above named property/land. We enclose for service   bundles each consisting of:—
(a) A sealed copy originating summons
(b) A copy of the Affidavit in support and its exhibits.
[where appropriate
(c) Order for abridgment of time and special directions
       dated   ]
Will you please arrange to serve these as soon as possible. When doing so, you should particularly note the following:

[*Where the application relates to residential premises and the Defendants are all named*]
1. You should attempt to locate and identify each person named and serve them by handing them the documents in the normal way. If after reasonable enquiry all or some of the Defendants cannot be found, then a bundle of the documents should be placed in an envelope addressed to the person or persons concerned and left at the premises.

2. [*Add where there are unnamed Defendants*]
    You will see that [in addition to the named Defendants] there are [also] unnamed Defendants. As well as effecting service as requested above, will you please place a bundle of documents inside a transparent envelope addressed to 'the occupiers' seal it and fix it to the main door or other conspicuous part of the premises and insert another bundle, similarly enclosed and addressed, through the letterbox of the premises, if there is one.

3. [*Where the application relates to land and the Defendants are named*]
    You should attempt to locate and identify each named

Defendant and effect service in the normal way by handing over the documents. If after enquiry you cannot find any named Defendants, please place the appropriate number of bundles in sealed envelopes addressed to the person or persons concerned and fix them to a post or tree at a prominent place on the land.

4. [*Add where there are unnamed Defendants*]
[In addition to service on named Defendants] please effect service by placing bundles of documents in sealed, transparent, envelopes addressed to 'the Occupiers' and fastening these firmly to stakes in the ground at prominent parts of the site. Our Client thinks that   will be sufficient. We shall be required to satisfy the Court that enough posts and bundles have been put up to bring the proceedings to the notice of the occupiers.

5. [*Add any special instructions arising from special directions for service – see eg precedent 13 above*]

6. [*Add where appropriate*]
In view of the numbers of people at the site, we strongly recommend that your attendance be accompanied by the Police. Please contact [*give details of name, station and telephone number*]. Please also note that under no circumstances should you persist with attempts at service if to do so would put your safety at risk.

7. If you would like our Client to attend with you to help identify the site/premises, please contact him at [*give details*].

8. [*Add in all cases*]
The requirements as to service are very precise. Please note the time when service starts and finishes and record all events and conversations on the premises/site in detail. Also, the sequence and manner of service should

be carefully recorded and all relevant information given to us for incorporation in the Affidavit of service that we will prepare for you to swear. Kindly note that in order to allow for the necessary number of clear days to elapse between service and the hearing, the papers in this matter must be served by not later than   next.
Yours faithfully,

15. DRAFT AFFIDAVIT OF SERVICE

[*Heading as in summons/application*]
AFFIDAVIT OF JAMES ERIC DODD

I, JAMES ERIC DODD, of Snoopers House, Melchester, Wessex, process server, HEREBY MAKE OATH and SAY as follows:

1. Acting on the instructions of the Plaintiff's Solicitors herein, I did on the   day of   attend at [address] for the purpose of serving the following documents on the Defendants in this action:
(a) A sealed copy of the Originating Summons [Originating application and notice of proceedings] dated
(b) A copy of the Affidavit of   sworn on the   and the exhibits referred to
[where appropriate
(c) The order of this Court dated   ]

2. I arrived at the property/site at   [and was accompanied by Sgt.   of the Wessex Constabulary whom I had met by previous arrangement]. On arrival I enquired for the named Defendants herein. The Defendants [*name them*] identified themselves to me and I effected service of the said documents by handing them copies. I was informed that the Defendant [*name*] was away and it was not known when she would return. Accordingly, I placed a bundle of the said documents in an envelope addressed to her which I then sealed and left in a prominent position [*specify*]. I also asked the person whom I met to ensure that [*name*] was told of my visit and of the papers left for her. I was assured that this would be done. [*Where there are large numbers of named Defendants a detailed but concise account of the manner of service should be given*].

[*For residential property*]
3. With regard to the unnamed Defendants, I placed a

bundle of the said documents inside a transparent envelope addressed to the occupiers which I then sealed and affixed to the main door of the premises. Another bundle in a sealed transparent envelope addressed to 'the occupiers' I inserted through the letter-box of the premises.

[For land]
4. With regard to the unnamed Defendants, before arrival at the site, I had placed   bundles of the said documents in transparent envelopes which I had sealed and addressed to 'the occupiers'. These I had firmly affixed to stout posts. I placed these in the ground at points at what I judged to be prominent points on the site. Because of the hostile attitude of the persons I found on the site, I was not able to go to the part of the site furthest from its entrance. I was advised by the Police Officers accompanying me not to do so.

OR
4. Because of the general hostility prevailing at the site *[particularize]* I judged that it was unwise to try to enter the site at all. I therefore placed   stakes with the said envelope attached in the ground at the edge of the site. I verily believe that under all the circumstances I did all I could to bring the notice of these proceedings to the attention of the Defendants.

[where appropriate]
5. In order to comply with the special directions for service detailed in the order of this Court dated
                    [then specify what was done]

6. I completed service [so far as I was able] at
and then left the premises/site.
[Sworn]

16. DRAFT AFFIDAVIT IN SUPPORT OF EX PARTE APPLICATION FOR LEAVE TO ISSUE WRIT/WARRANT OF RESTITUTION[9]

[*Heading as in summons/application*]
I, MICHAEL WILLIAMS of The Council Offices, Melchester, Wessex, HEREBY MAKE OATH and SAY as follows:

1. This Affidavit is sworn by me in support of an application for leave to issue a Writ/Warrant of Restitution. On this Court made an order for possession in these proceedings. A Writ/Warrant of Possession was subsequently issued and execution effected on   .

2. On   I became aware of a re-occupation of the property. When I visited the property, I recognised one man whose name I do not know, as being one of those who was previously in it OR I told the persons I found in the property that it was already covered by a Court Order for possession. The person to whom I spoke told me he knew of the existence of the Order, but if I went to Court he would deny all knowledge of it [OR set out whatever circumstances the Plaintiff relies on to establish a sufficient nexus between the circumstances of the original trespass and that now occurring]

3. Under all the circumstances, I verily believe that the persons now trespassing on the property are part of the group doing so when the original order was made. I therefore respectfully seek leave to issue a Writ/Warrant of restitution.
[*Sworn*]

---

9. See *Wiltshire County Council v Frazer (No 2)* [1986] 1 All ER 65; [1986] 1 WLR 109.

The summary procedure under the Caravan Sites Act 1968, Part II

1. The summary procedure under the Caravan Sites Act 1968, Part II
2. Draft complaint under the Caravan Sites Act 1968, s 11
3. Draft summons
4. Order on complaint

The procedure created by Part II of this Act, the relevant sections of which are set out below, is wholly distinct from the civil procedure for the summary possession of land considered in the main part of this book. Nevertheless, it has certain similarities in that it has few formalities by way of pleadings; it may be used against unnamed defendants; and the procedures for service are precise and, if not followed, may result in the failure of the proceedings brought under it. Its essential feature is that it is only available to local authorities against gipsies.

The procedure is not well known nor commonly used. However, in circumstances where it can be invoked, it may provide a swift and effective remedy and is thus included in this book, with a few notes of explanation, for those practitioners who find themselves with a set of circumstances coming within it.

The Caravan Sites Act 1968, s 10 as amended by the Criminal Justice Act 1982, ss 38 and 46, provides:

10. Prohibition of unauthorised camping in designated areas

(1) In any area designated under the following pro-

visions of this Act as an area to which this section applies it shall be an offence for any person being a gipsy to station a caravan for the purpose of residing for any period—

(*a*)   on any land situated within the boundaries of a highway, or

(*b*)   on any other unoccupied land, or

(*c*)   on any occupied land without the consent of the occupier.

(2)   In proceedings against any person for an offence under this section it shall be a defence to prove that the caravan was stationed on the land in consequence of illness, mechanical breakdown or other immediate emergency and that he removed it (or intended to remove it) as soon as reasonably practicable.

(3)   Any person guilty of an offence under this section shall be liable on summary conviction to a fine not exceeding level 1 on the standard scale; and if the offence of which he is convicted is continued after the conviction he shall be guilty of a further offence and shall be liable in respect thereof to a fine not exceeding £5 for every day on which the offence is so continued.

Sections 11 and 12 as substituted by the Local Government, Planning and Land Act 1980, ss 174 and 175 respectively and as amended by the Local Government Act 1985, s 16, Sch 8, para 11(2) now provide:

11. Orders for removal of unlawfully parked caravans and their occupants

(1)   In any area to which section 10 of this Act applies, a magistrates' court may, on a complaint made by a local authority, and if satisfied that a caravan is stationed on land within that authority's area in contravention of that section, make an order requiring any caravan (whether or not identified in the order) which is so stationed on the land to be removed together with any person residing in it.

(2) An order under this section may authorise the local authority to take such steps as are reasonably necessary to ensure that the order is complied with and in particular, may authorise the authority, by its officers and servants—

(*a*) to enter upon the land specified in the order; and

(*b*) to take, in relation to any caravan to be removed pursuant to the order, such steps for securing entry and rendering it suitable for removal as may be so specified.

(3) The local authority shall not enter upon any occupied land unless they have given to the owner and occupier at least 24 hours' notice of their intention to do so, or unless after reasonable inquiries they are unable to ascertain their names and addresses.

(4) A person who intentionally obstructs any person acting in the exercise of any power conferred on him by an order under this section shall be guilty of an offence and liable on summary conviction to a fine not exceeding level 3 on the standard scale.

(5) [Repealed by the Police and Criminal Evidence Act 1984, ss 26(1), 119(2), Sch 7].

(6) Where a complaint is made under this section, a summons issued by the court requiring the person or persons to whom it is directed to appear before the court to answer to the complaint may be directed—

(*a*) to the occupant of a particular caravan stationed on the land in question, or

(*b*) to all occupants of caravans stationed there, without naming him or them.

(7) Where it is impracticable to serve such a summons on a person named in it, it shall be treated as duly served on him if a copy of it is fixed in a prominent place to the caravan concerned; and where such a summons is directed to the unnamed occupants of caravans, it shall be treated as duly served on those occupants if a copy of it is fixed in a prominent place to every

caravan stationed on the land in question at the time when service is thus effected.

(8) The local authority shall take such steps as may be reasonably practicable to secure that a copy of any such summons is displayed on the land in question (otherwise than by being fixed to a caravan) in a manner designed to ensure that it is likely to be seen by any person camping on the land.

(9) Notice of any such summons shall be given by the local authority to the owner of the land in question and to any occupier of that land unless, after reasonable inquiries, the authority is unable to ascertain the name and address of the owner or occupier; and the owner of any such land and any occupier of any such land shall be entitled to appear and to be heard in the proceedings.

(10) Section 55(2) of the Magistrates' Courts Act 1980 (warrant for arrest of defendant failing to appear) does not apply to proceedings on a complaint made under this section.

12. Designation of areas

(1) Subject to subsection (3) below, the Minister may by order made on the application of the council of a county, metropolitan district or London borough council designate the area of that council as an area to which section 10 of this Act applies.

(2) Subject to subsection (3) below, the Minister may by order made on the joint application of a county council and one or more councils of districts within that county designate the area of the district or, as the case may be, the combined areas of the districts, as an area to which section 10 of this Act applies.

(2A) Subject to subsection (3) below, the Minister may by order made on the joint application of two or more metropolitan district councils designate the area of those councils as an area to which section 10 of this Act applies.

(3) The Minister shall not make an order under subsection (1), (2) or (2A) above in respect of any area unless it appears to him either that adequate provision is made in the area for the accommodation of gipsies residing in or resorting to the area, or that in all the circumstances it is not necessary or expedient to make any such provision.

(4) An order under this section may be revoked by an order made by the Minister, either on the application of the authority or authorities which made the original application or without such an application.

(5) The power of the Minister to make orders under this section shall be exercisable by statutory instrument; and any statutory instrument made by virtue of this section shall be subject to annulment in pursuance of a resolution of either House of Parliament.

(6) Where an order under this section is made in respect of any area it shall be the duty of the county council for that area or, as the case may be, the metropolitan district council or councils or the London borough council concerned to take such steps as are reasonably practicable to inform gipsies within the area of the making and effect of the order.

Definitions

'Gipsies' means by s 16 'persons of nomadic habit of life, whatever their race or origin, but does not include members of organized groups of travelling showmen or of persons engaged in travelling circuses travelling together as such'.

'Caravan' has the meaning assigned to it by Part I of the Caravan Site and Control of Development Act 1960, s 29, namely 'any structure designed or adapted for human habitation which is capable of being moved from one place to another (whether by being towed, or by being transported on a motor vehicle or trailer) and any motor vehicle so designed or adapted, but does not include:

(a) any railway rolling stock which is for the time being on rails forming part of a railway system, or
(b) any tent'.

Need for a designation order

Before the procedure created by s 11 can be invoked, it is essential that a designation order under s 12 shall be in force in relation to the area in which any occupied land is situated. Such a designation order is made by statutory instrument.

Essential conditions for complaint to be made

If such an order is in force, consideration must then be given to s 10(1). This creates an offence, punishable in accordance with s 10(3) where any person, being a gipsy, stations in an area to which s 10 has been applied by an order made under s 12, a caravan, for the purpose of residing in it, for any period:
(a) on any land situated within the boundaries of a highway, or
(b) on any other unoccupied land,[1] or
(c) on any land occupied without the consent of the occupier.
S 10(2) sets out the defences available to such a person.

We are not here concerned with the prosecution of persons for any criminal offence, but it will have been noted that before the possession procedure of s 11 may be invoked, the offence conditions of s 10 must apply.

If those conditions apply, then by s 11(1) a local authority may make a complaint to a magistrates' court for an order requiring any caravan (whether or not identified in the order)

---

1. Land is not 'unoccupied' for the purposes of s 10(1)(b) if a gipsy enters with the consent of the owner to carry out acts preparatory to stationing a caravan, such as the erection of fences: *R v Beaconsfield Justices, ex p Stubbings* (1987) Times, 17 April.

which is stationed on the land to be removed, together with any person residing in it.

See below, pages 131–133 for a suitable form of complaint and summons.

The procedure generally

For the most part, s 11 is self-explanatory, but the following points should be noted:

1. Although the complaint must be made by a local authority, the procedure is not restricted to local authority land. By s 11(3) where land is not the local authority's, the authority may not enter occupied land unless they have given the owner and occupier at least 24 hours notice, unless after reasonable enquiries they are unable to ascertain the names and addresses of the owner or occupier.

2. Section 11(6) contains provisions enabling the summons issued pursuant to the complaint to be served whether or not the names of occupiers are known.

3. Section 11(7) contains service provisions which are similar to Order 113, rule 4, but not identical. Section 11(8) imposes a further obligation on the complainant to display a copy of the summons on the land in question in a manner designed to ensure that it is likely to be seen by any person camping on the land. This is a requirement, whether or not personal service has been effected, as prescribed by s 11(7).

4. Notice of the summons must be given to the owner 'and occupier' of the land unless after reasonable enquiries the local authority is unable to discover the name and address of

the occupier (s 11(9)). The reference to 'the occupier' is not to a person against whom an order for possession is sought.

At the hearing of the summons, a proper copy of the designation order under s 12 must be produced. Oral evidence shall be given of the facts of the occupation and of the local authority's contention that the persons in occupation are gipsies and what they occupy are caravans. Oral evidence must be given that notice has been given to the owner or occupier of the land, or that enquiries have been made to ascertain their identity and that these have failed.

Evidence must also be given that none of the defences set out in s 10(2) is available to any person in occupation of the land.

Particular attention should be paid to the provisions as to service and the person giving evidence should be taken carefully through each stage of service (the comments in Chapter 8 above about service may be found useful in this regard.)

As this is a sparsely used procedure, the magistrates may wish to have substantial assistance, particularly in relation to the sort of order they should make, having regard to their powers under s 11(2). A suggested form of order is on page 134, below. Enforcement of the order for possession is a matter for the complainant. Any directions given by the court in the order must be complied with. By s 11(4) it is an offence intentionally to obstruct any person acting in the exercise of any power conferred on him by an order made by the court.

A party aggrieved by an order under s 11 should appeal by way of case stated rather than bring proceedings for judicial review.[2]

---

2. *R v Beaconsfield Justices, ex p Stubbings* ibid, per Woolf LJ.

DRAFT COMPLAINT UNDER THE CARAVAN SITES ACT 1968, SECTION 11

In the Melchester Magistrates' Court   (Code   )
The Magistrates' Court Act 1980, s 51, Magistrates' Court Rules 1981, Rule 4.

DATE	:	
DEFENDANTS	:	*[List any names and all [other] persons in caravans/vehicles stationed at [address]*
MATTER OF COMPLAINT	:	WHEREAS the Defendants being gipsies did on in an area to which Section 10 of the Caravan Sites Act 1968 applies station caravans/vehicles on land situated within the County of Wessex namely on land known as in the said County in contravention of the said Section 10. The Melchester District Council DO HEREBY COMPLAIN that an order be made by the Melchester Magistrates' Court under Section 11 of the Caravan Sites Act 1968 (as amended by Section 174 of the Local Government Planning and Land Act 1980) requiring the said caravans/vehicles to be removed by the Defendants together with any person residing in them AND that it be further ordered that the Melchester District

Council be authorised to take such steps as are reasonably necessary to ensure that the first mentioned Order is complied with and in particular that the said Melchester District Council by its servants and officers be authorised to take in relation to the said caravans/vehicles to be removed pursuant to the said order such steps for securing entry and rendering them suitable for removal as may be specified by the Court

THE COMPLAINT OF   :   [*Name of appropriate officer*]
                                on behalf of Melchester
                                District Council
                                [*address*]

Telephone   :

who states that the Defendants were responsible for the matter of complaint of which particulars are given above.

....

TAKEN BEFORE ME

....

Justices Clerk

DRAFT SUMMONS

In the Melchester Magistrates' Court   (Code   )
The Magistrates' Court Act 1980, s 51, Magistrates' Court
Rules 1981, rule 4.

DATE   :

TO THE DEFENDANTS   : All   persons   in   caravans/
                                        vehicles
                                        at
                                        Melchester, Wessex

YOU ARE HEREBY SUMMONED TO APPEAR on   the
        day of   at   o'clock before the
Magistrates' Court at   to answer the following
Complaint

MATTER OF COMPLAINT
[then following the wording of the Complaint as in previous
precedent].

The Complainant is   :
Date of Complaint   :

                            . . . .
                                  Justices Clerk

ORDER ON COMPLAINT

Petty Sessional Division of Melchester
Date   :
Defendant/Address   :   *[Any named Defendants and]* all
                                    persons   in   caravans/vehicles
                                    stationed at [address]
On the Complaint of   :
Complainant   :
Address   :   Melchester District Council
                                    [address]
that

MATTER OF COMPLAINT

WHEREAS   the Defendants being gipsies did on   in
an area to which Section 10 of the Caravan Sites
Act 1968 applies station caravans/vehicles on
land situated within the County of Wessex,
namely on *[specify land]* AND the Melchester
District Council having COMPLAINED that
an Order be made by the Melchester Magistrates Court under Section 11 of the Caravan
Sites Act 1968 (as amended by Section 174 of
the Local Government Planning and Land Act
1980) requiring the said caravans/vehicles to be
removed by the Defendants together with any
persons residing in them
IT IS ADJUDGED that the COMPLAINT is true and it
is ORDERED that
The said Council by its officers and servants are
hereby authorised to enter upon the said land at
in the County of Wessex and remove
the said caravans/vehicles AND it is further
ordered that the Melchester District Council be
authorised to take such steps as are reasonably
necessary to ensure that the first mentioned
order is complied with.
By order of the Court

Index